GROWING THE SMALLER CHURCH

Other titles in the CPAS Handbook Series

A CPAS Handbook

GROWING THE SMALLER CHURCH

Mike Breen
with Simon Fox

Series Editor: Paul Simmonds

Marshall Pickering
An Imprint of HarperCollins*Publishers*

Marshall Pickering is an imprint of
HarperCollins*Religious*,
Part of HarperCollins*Publishers*,
77–85 Fulham Palace Road, London W6 8JB

First published in Great Britain
in 1992 by Marshall Pickering

1 3 5 7 9 10 8 6 4 2

The Author asserts the moral right to
be identified as the author of this work

A catalogue record for this book is
available from the British Library

ISBN 0 551 02372 4

Printed and bound in Great Britain by
HarperCollinsManufacturing Glasgow

To the People and Parish
of All Saints

Contents

Introduction

Why grow?

This book is *not* about turning small congregations into large ones. Nevertheless is is about numerical growth. It is as well said of churches as it is of people: if you do not grow you will eventually die.

So often church growth is associated with pictures of burgeoning congregations. But the Great Commission was never: "Go and proclaim the Gospel from the large churches . . ." Indeed frontier evangelism invariably finds itself working with small struggling churches. This was true of the missionary movement of the last century and of the emerging churches in New Testament times. Yet from those small bases came a substantial and widespread evangelization.

Sometimes growth seems such a vain hope, especially in the kind of church where one family moving can leave a great gap, or where the congreation struggles to maintain a building designed for ten times their number. Yet if the church in Britain is to stop declining, it is the small churches which hold the key. So, read on!

What is special about the smaller church?

While the large and very large churches often capture the headlines, over half the people who attend church find themselves in a church which has seventy people or fewer at the main service. Eight out of ten worshippers are in a congregation with under 120 people.

Soon after the results of the 1989 church census were published

I needed to discover the size of the average church. The results suggest this is around ninety Sunday attenders – but that includes both evening and morning congregations. It is probably fair to conclude that if your Sunday morning congregation is around seventy or fewer you are in a smaller than average church. Surprisingly, it is a similar picture in the United States, despite the media profile of the mega-churches.

A small church is likely to be one where you can know most of the people. It is a place where people are missed if they are absent for a prolonged period, and where the whole church shares in the sufferings and joys of individual members and families. It is in the small church that people can have a close relationship with the minister and others in leadership.

Some of the problems of the small church are to do with resources. The difficulties often arise because the programmes and expectations of many small churches are modelled on the experiences of much larger congregations. But this is a mismatch of vision with reality.

First of all, there are fewer people in the small church, yet it is assumed that the same range of activities ought to be sustained. This results in a dilution of effort or an excessive workload on a few. Stopping activities which have come to the end of their useful life is hard, and is often deferred indefinitely, diverting energy from the main enterprise.

Second, the *proportion* of church members needed to make any activity viable, is higher than in a large church. For example, suppose you decide to run a short training course on "The Christian Living in a Secular Society", with a speaker from a neighbouring church. In a church with a membership of fifty, if only three people turn up to your course you feel disappointed and cancel the event. If you run the same thing in a church with a membership of 500, and you get the same proportion of the membership, you will have a perfectly satisfactory group of thirty people.

Third, some routine maintenance tasks of administration take just as long for a small church as for a large one. This might include such diverse things as filling in forms for the church authorities, choosing the hymns for the services or reading diocesan mailings. A large church may have a full-time administrator or a number of full-time staff.

It is a similar picture with finances. Some of the fixed costs which do not depend on the size of the congregation may be equally the same for a small church as a large church. Heating costs and graveyard upkeep, for example, may be proportionately more of a burden to a small church.

I am demonstrating these points not because I believe we should move to having a few large churches rather than a lot of small ones, but to point out some of the differences and difficulties faced by the small church. Yet, as this book shows, the smaller church also has many advantages.

If you believe in the value of each Christian relating to three sizes of group – a *cell*, a *congregation* and a unit of *celebration* – as an important element in helping the church to grow, then we need to look at this in the context of the small church. A few churches are small enough to be a *cell*. Large churches fall into the category of *celebration*; they usually have a small group structure, but nothing in between. A small church can have all three sizes. As long as it has small groups of some kind, and members can get to a celebration event from time to time, the small church provides the *congregation* size unit at the main services.

Furthermore, we have to recognize the value of small churches in covering a large number of communities and functioning more effectively at a local level.

Small churches: the key to country-wide church growth

If we are to halt the decline in church attendance and membership it is the small churches which will be the most important. According to church growth experts, we must concentrate on helping the small churches to evangelize and grow. This is obvious once you realize that most church members belong to smaller churches. But, in addition, if we are to reach the maximum number of people, having a larger number of small Christian communities provides a Christian witness in every little population centre and local neighbourhood. This is vital, particularly in urban areas where church attendance is relatively low, as illustrated by some of the stories in this book.

This raises the spectre of lots of smaller churches becoming large churches, but still living with the structures and outlook of a small church. For the past few years in CPAS we have been running consultations (called "200 plus") with churches trying to cope with the change to large church status. Mike Breen has faced up to this in All Saints, and explains how, along with churches elsewhere, they have come to see the importance of valuing the small. They have split up into a number of small congregations. This may seem ironic to a vicar struggling to care for several small congregations (as in a rural situation). But perhaps there are lessons here in working towards a long-term goal, in which each congregation sees itself as part of a larger unit, doing away with some of the overlap and duplication. This book will help those approaching the question of growth from this standpoint.

How does it work?
So what happens when a small church grows? What plans need to be laid? Some churches grow by starting new congregations in the same building. Others, like the All Saints described in this book, have planted separate congregations around the parish.

In this way the small church shape and structure is retained, and there is a mechanism for continuous growth without a complete rethink everytime the church grows substantially. Furthermore, with multi-congregation churches *some* of the economies of scale of a large church begin to come into play. All Saints now has three congregations, which together total just 200. They hope to create further small congregations, but they will remain a single church across the community.

This book is a description of attempts to grow. It describes experiments not blueprints. But the pattern developed here reflects changes elsewhere in the Church. The outworking of the detail varies, but for Mike Breen there are two key principles of leadership which underpin the ministry described in this book.

Cultivating a growth mentality

There is no church, however small, which cannot grow in numbers – unless of course the entire neighbourhood attends! So the smallest church can contemplate and pray for growth. But it needs to become part of the bloodstream of the church. Unless we are willing to allow growth, nothing will happen.

Sometimes you wonder why a church does not grow. But when you talk to the members, you find no particular interest or desire for it. They do not object but neither do they think it very important. They are not motivated. All Saints chose to make growth a priority. Everyone got involved in finding out what they needed to do.

Listening to God

All the attempts at growth described in this book sprang from an attitude of listening to God, coupled with an openness to experimenting in faith. Rather than copying other churches straight, Mike describes how he had to learn to be willing to repent – in the sense of letting go the past and beginning afresh. This resulted in some unusual approaches to evangelism, pastoral care, worship, work in the community, youth work and so on. The danger is that others will simply try the ideas (which will date and be superceded). Rather, it is the approach which is important. It springs from praying for growth and being willing to be available to be fully part of the process. In a sense, this is the most important point which Mike Breen is trying to illustrate, namely, that learning to listen to God is the exciting responsibility of every minister and church leader.

Paul Simmonds
CPAS Handbook Series Editor

1

The Learning Loop

1.1 Stop, look and listen

No matter how often we admit our dependence on God in everything we do to build His Kingdom, the plain fact is that many of us carry on as if it were all down to us. This certainly used to be the case with me, but a particular incident in my life changed my whole outlook. Discovering who really was in control was painful – quite literally!

I had spent my first year after ordination as the curate at St Martin's, Cambridge. During the following year I continued working in Cambridge as the team leader of a youth and community centre called the Romsey Mill. Many of my hopes and expectations had remained unfulfilled. I had expected a greater response to the preaching of the Gospel; I had expected to see events like those recorded in the New Testament. I began to wonder what I had been called to do. I asked God to speak to me about these things.

A couple of years after being ordained as a minister in the Church of England I was cutting the grass in the back garden of our family home. I came across two large ant nests. I knew I would have to get rid of them, because our first child, Rebecca, had just started to walk, and these ants would be one of the first things she would come across in the garden. Rather unwisely, I decided to pour petrol on the nests and set light to them! Not surprisingly, I thus not only destroyed the nests but also succeeded in setting light to my trousers! My legs were badly burned and I was taken to hospital. The surgeons removed the burned skin and then I had to wait for the condition of my legs to stabilize so that skin grafts could be applied to the injured areas. Lying there in my hospital bed, I felt lonely and depressed – feelings I was not accustomed to. The days seemed endless, punctuated only by the visits of the nurses. It was a very trying time. However, God was using the difficulty and pain of my situation to turn me around and change my life. I began to question what I was doing and where I was going.

Although I knew how to ask the questions, I didn't know how to get the answers. Before I could hear from God I had to be alone and at a standstill. Forced into inactivity by the accident with the petrol, I began to notice a number of things. First, as I prayed it seemed as though God was saying over and over again, "Let me do it". The books I read while in hospital seemed to be saying the same thing, as did a tape recording of John Wimber's testimony which I listened to.

As I convalesced, I realized that something fundamental had happened to me: my self-reliance had been shattered and a new awareness of God's presence had taken its place. New desires began to fill my mind. Worship, which had always been something of a chore to me, began to come alive. I would sit for hours listening to worship tapes, singing along and trying to reproduce the tunes as I learned to play the guitar. A new, urgent desire to proclaim the Gospel captivated me, and a wish to hear God speak to me was rekindled. The turn-around in my life had begun. I can best sum up this period in my life in three words: **stop, look and listen:**

Stop:	I had to cease all my activity before I could hear God's answer.
Look:	I had honestly to appraise my own effectiveness before any changes could be made.
Listen:	I had to listen with a determination to obey.

After a revelation like this it was difficult getting back into my work. It was hard to get the balance right between doing adequate planning and allowing God space to act. But gradually my wife, Sally, and I and the rest of the Romsey Mill team learned how to do it, and we began to see some remarkable results. Many young people and adults became Christians, and we saw many healed and released from deep spiritual bondage. In many ways the events that took place were an outward sign of what was going on inside me and other members of the team. Other people were released into worship as we were taken into new dimensions in our personal devotions. Evangelism flourished as we realized that we were ourselves recipients of God's mercy. New methods of outreach and training were pioneered as we were taken further in our own discipleship. God was planting the seeds of His Kingdom in us and bringing forth fruit in its time. The seeds that were planted then are still producing a crop in my everyday experience today. Some of this crop can be seen in the lives of others, and some of it has been planted back into the soil of my own life for a future harvest.

After two years of learning that the power and presence of God is as real now as in New Testament times, Sally and I knew that God was leading us to take up the next calling of our lives – the inner city. We spent some time thinking and praying about what God was calling us to, and wrote down a basic profile of the sort of church and area we should go to next.

After this we began to apply for jobs throughout the country, asking God to reveal where we should go. We were invited to a number of positions, all of which fulfilled many of our hopes and desires, but none of them seemed to be the place for us. When we came to meet the leaders of All Saints Church, Brixton Hill, we experienced a mixed bag of emotions. On the one hand, it was the most difficult of all the situations we had considered; on the other hand, I felt the greatest peace about it. Wisely, Sally suggested that we should let it rest on our minds for a while to see whether God would say any more.

We had decided to ask some close friends, Malcolm and Chris Wylie, to help us with the decision-making process. We knew that they would pray and offer wise counsel. Chris believed that God had given her a passage from Scripture for us, but was unsure of its application. She decided to read it to us when we next met. The passage was Hebrews 10:32–39:

> Remember those earlier days after you had received the light, when you stood your ground in a great contest in the face of suffering. Sometimes you were publicly exposed to insult and persecution; at other times you stood side by side with those who were so treated. You sympathized with those in prison and joyfully accepted the confiscation of your property, because you knew that you yourselves had better and lasting possessions.
>
> So do not throw away your confidence: it will be richly rewarded. You need to persevere so that when you have done the will of God, you will receive what He has promised. For in just a very little while, "He who is coming will come and will not delay. But My righteous one will live by faith. And if he shrinks back, I will not be pleased with him." But we are not of those who shrink back and are destroyed, but of those who believe and are saved.

As Chris read this passage it reminded Sally and me of our past experiences – becoming Christians, receiving God's call to work for Him, and many other things. The passage seemed to be describing all this.

After Chris had finished we both knew for certain that God had spoken and that through this passage and through our two friends He had called us to All Saints. Sally had been less sure than I that All Saints was the right place for us, but the passage came to her as a strong confirmation. No one had tried to convince her; she had heard God for herself. Since then we have often re-read this passage, and we have always been impressed by the fact that it seems both to speak about our past and to foretell our future.

1.2 The Learning Loop

The experience of going into hospital, seeking God's guidance and being led to All Saints was all part of what is now a familiar process in my life. I have been through it time and again. I call it "the Learning Loop". It is the process by which, through deeper repentance and greater faith, we learn new things from God.

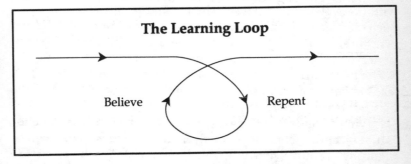

We go through this loop of repentance and faith for the first time when we become Christians, and subsequently we need to go through it again and again. I had to go through the loop before God could use me at All Saints. During my time there it has been important not only in my own life but also in the life of the whole church.

Jesus made it clear that repentance and faith are all that we need to enter the Kingdom of God. He said, "The time has come. The Kingdom of God is near. Repent and believe the good news!" (Mark 1:15). Repentance, as I understand it now, is a process, not simply an event; it is a process which is intended to lead us to genuine accountability to God. Faith is also a process – one by which we act on what we believe God to be saying and make a place in our lives for Him to do what He chooses. As I have reflected on repentance and faith I have been led to the conclusion that God wants us to enter into them continuously.

It seems to me that within repentance there are three basic

things to be done. First there needs to be honest **observation** of what has been done, said or thought. Seeing things as they are is very important if we are to change and become the people God wants us to be.

After observation comes **review**. This is a weighing of our lives and a judging of our effectiveness. Again, this needs to be done with honesty if we are to see change and progress in our lives. Such observation and review need to be carried out in the light of Scripture, with the counsel of others and through our own understanding of what is taking place in our lives.

The third part of the process of repentance is **discussion**. This leads to genuine accountability, so that any blinkers to reality we may be wearing are removed.

Having repented in this way, we can then start to believe for future action. Belief also involves three stages. First comes **planning**. I think this is a much underrated activity in the Church. It is a vital and basic function of Christian discipleship. The whole process of planning is discussed at more length in Chapter 3.

As well as planning we need to build **communication** into the process of belief. We need to ask ourselves who else needs to know about the plan.

Thirdly, there must be **action**. If a plan does not result in action it is just a waste of time!

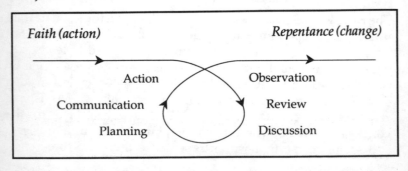

Faith (action)   Repentance (change)

Action   Observation

Communication   Review

Planning   Discussion

The Learning Loop has been a crucial part of our work at All Saints. Through it God has taught us specific lessons about specific situations, and has revealed to us ways of doing things which we would otherwise never have thought of. The programmes described in this book came out of this learning process. The programmes themselves may not necessarily be translatable to other parishes, but the process of learning which gave them birth is relevant to all churches.

Here is the Learning Loop expressed with relevance to the local church situation:

The Learning Loop and the local church

Repentance/change

● Observe – get all the facts about the church's situation.

● Review – think through and weigh up the facts in order to gain understanding.

● Discuss – talk things over with people in the church so as to reach greater clarity.

Faith/action

● Plan – make decisions about what needs to change and what needs to be done.

● Communicate – share the vision for the future with others in the church and involve them in it.

● Act – get on and do what God has told you to do.

1.3   Grit and pearls

Being a disciple of Jesus is costly; it involves pain. Jesus stated this truth very clearly: "If anyone would come after Me, he must deny himself and take up his cross and follow Me. For whoever wants to save his life will lose it, but whoever loses his life for Me will save it" (Matthew 16:24–25).

The formation of a pearl in an oyster shell is for me a picture which very helpfully illustrates both the growth and the pain involved in working for the Kingdom of God. A pearl is formed when grit gets into the oyster shell. The pain and irritation which the grit causes make the oyster secrete a substance which forms a pearl around the grit, softening its edges and creating out of it something of lasting beauty and worth. Although this process is not described in detail by Jesus, He does speak of the Kingdom as a pearl of great value (Matthew 13:45–46). In another place He describes the Kingdom as a collection of pearls, which the disciples should not cast before swine (Matthew 7:6).

In my experience God brings forth His Kingdom through the pain and irritation which we suffer in our lives (see Acts 14:22). Pain of one sort or another – spiritual, emotional or physical (i.e. sickness) – is used. It seems as if God chooses to place grit in our shells, so that He can create something of value from our lives. This book tells the story of how God used grit to produce the pearls of His Kingdom in my life and in the lives of those I know and serve at All Saints. As you read about our experiences, please remember that it is probably better for God to place grit in your shell than for you simply to borrow our pearls.

The Learning Loop becomes a continuous process throughout the life of an individual or a church. One loop leads on to another, so that the result is a string of Kingdom "pearls".

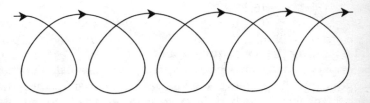

2

The Right Questions and Answers

2.1 Asking the right questions

Before any evangelism begins, preparation is essential. It's no use working out all the answers before we know what the questions are! Evangelism which is inappropriate and fails to produce results is exhausting and disheartening, and so it is of primary importance to find out what are the real needs of the community which the local church serves. This is especially important for those churches which draw the majority of their members from outlying areas.

There is only one way to find out what is happening in a community, and that is to spend time talking with and listening to the people who live there. All Saints was already doing this when I arrived as the new vicar. Many of its members had lived on Brixton Hill all their lives. For example, a pressing need which they had recognized was that some sort of youth work should be started. But the young people were only one group in the community, and we needed to know about all the others too.

Soon after I arrived some of the church members and I surveyed and audited the area. We spent a number of wet winter Saturday afternoons looking at every house, shop and block of flats in the parish. We were looking at the buildings to see if they could tell us anything about the area and the people who lived in it. We were looking for signs of poverty and deprivation, wealth and prosperity. We spoke to hundreds of people, using a community questionnaire. We hoped that by doing this we would come to know what was happening locally. We also used a congregational questionnaire which focused mainly on the gifts and expectations of the church members, but also on their perceptions of the needs of the community. In addition to all this we asked a number of church members – young, old, male, female, black, white – to keep a diary for several weeks so that we could see the obstacles, difficulties, opportunities and joys that the congregation experienced in their everyday lives. This was one of many occasions when the *stop-look-listen* formula applied:

- We had to *stop* – and find the time to look and listen. All Saints as a whole had to put its activities "on hold".

- We had to *look* – to find out what was happening in the community. We had to observe carefully.

- We had to *listen* – to ensure that our response was appropriate. We had to listen to the community and to God.

2.2 Praise and Litter Marches

As we brought all this information together a picture began to emerge. Some of the findings were predictable. Heavy burdens of deprivation and poverty were borne by the mothers, the children, the unemployed and the black people in the community. But there were some surprises too. People living in the parish were asked to name the three best things and the three worst things about it. The worst thing which polled the most votes was the litter and rubbish on the streets. We had expected problems such as street violence, crime, poor housing and inadequate local amenities to be at the top of the "worst things" list. However, when we double-checked by asking others directly whether they saw street litter and rubbish as a problem, the overwhelming response was "Yes".

At first we had no idea how to respond to this need, but as we thought and prayed it through, an idea began to develop. Praise marches, following the *Make Way* theme, were becoming popular all around the country. We thought it might be a good idea if we marched and cleared up the litter at the same time. The worship group recorded a dozen or so songs, and during the march these were played on a "ghetto blaster" which was pushed around on a pram decorated with balloons. This left everyone's hands free to pick up litter. Everyone taking part was supplied with a dustbin liner and a plastic glove; some brought brooms and shovels. As we walked on our prearranged route around the parish we sang as loudly as we could and cleared the streets as we went!

The day after the march you could tell where the church had been. Where we had worshipped and sung the praises of God the streets were clean. Of course, they got dirty again, but something important about the Kingdom had been demonstrated in the community.

That was the first Praise and Litter March, and we have since then held many others during the summer months. On occasions we have singled out particular areas such as the courtyard in front of a block of flats. The response has always been positive and has often led to opportunities to talk about the Kingdom of God. Some residents have brought us drinks and biscuits as we have cleaned their streets or courtyards; others have been visibly moved by what they have seen us doing. By this activity we are not seeking to promote or publicize ourselves; rather, we are trying to demonstrate that we believe in God's Good News.

Some would ask what is the long-term benefit of such a programme. This is difficult to answer directly. What is certain is that a parable of the Kingdom is being acted out before the eyes of the watching community every time we clean the streets.

2.3　Care and Repair

If litter was one of the problems in the community, housing was another major area of concern which our audit, questionnaires

---

Praise and Litter March checklist

- Plan the route (choosing areas where the March will have the most effect).

- Inform the police (for traffic control and authorization of the route).

- Choose the songs (record them on a cassette or get your worship group to practise them).

- Buy some plastic sacks and gloves.

- Provide any other necessary tools or equipment (shovels, brooms, etc.).

- Ensure that everyone taking part knows when and where the March is taking place.

- Ensure that you have a good method of reporting the results to the whole church, so that those doing the work can be encouraged and supported.

---

and other fact-finding exercises revealed. Obviously, with our limited resources there was little we could do about the many chronic and intractable problems surrounding us, but we were able to take constructive action in some ways. We began a Care and Repair programme which helped people with household repairs and decorating. We began with needs we knew existed in our own congregation and among their friends, neighbours and wider families. The Care and Repair team leader, who was a church worker, organized a small team of helpers and set about this very practical demonstration of the church's concern for the community it served.

Door and window locks were fitted, rooms were decorated,

carpets were laid and hoovers were fixed. Usually we supplied the skills and labour, which the people supplied the cost of materials. Where this was not possible we simply trusted that our resources would stretch to pay for any essential costs that might be incurred. We made the elderly and single parents our priority because these people seemed to be the most vulnerable and the least able to help themselves in these particular areas of need.

One old lady, who was contacted initially through a conversation on the street, revealed that she was depressed about the state of the decoration of her flat. She said it made her feel quite desperate at times. We went to see her flat and arranged with her a time when we would return with a team of painters. She was so encouraged that by the time the team arrived a few days later, she had stripped the wallpaper from her hall and had prepared the room for painting. After painting the hall the team agreed to return to do the sitting room. When they came to do this job they found that she had enlisted the help of her neighbours and had half-completed the task herself. Her whole disposition seemed to change and she became much more positive about her home and her life in general.

In our situation, we initiated Care and Repair through a full-time member of the pastoral team who was seconded part-time to this work and part-time to youth work. When it was up and running it was handed over and is now maintained informally through our small-group network. There is much to be said for a full-timer who sets up a project, ensures its smooth running, and then passes it on. This means that new projects can be constantly developed and as they are handed over a fresh wave of ideas and enthusiasm is injected. A full-timer can put his or her energies into overcoming the obstacles that almost always arise when something new is being created, and when early difficulties are ironed out, others can share in the leadership. This is a pattern which we have followed in much of our youth and community work.

Care and Repair checklist

- Identify people to initiate the project and co-ordinate the work in the area.

- Establish a method of referral. Begin with the needs known to the congregation and work among their family and friends. Encourage publicity through word of mouth so that you work out from established relationships to the people beyond.

- Establish a reliable method of inspecting and then carrying out repairs (e.g. housegroups to serve their immediate localities or special Care and Repair task groups). It is vitally important not to let people down on dates, quality of workmanship and so on.

- Establish a method of ensuring continuing caring contact (e.g. housegroups, pastoral visits).

- Make provision for some limited financial reserve, out of which the cost of special needs can be met.

2.4 "Street Level" – All Saints' shop

As we identified areas of need in the community we longed to make advice, help and simple counselling available to people. The problem was: how could we make it possible for people to obtain the help they needed? We decided as a church to establish a point of contact with the community other than our own building on Lyham Road. To do this we purchased the lease for a shop in the main shopping area of Brixton Hill. Over the years a number of projects have been based here. In setting up this high street location we needed to be sure that certain things were built into our approach from the beginning.

We realized that if a church offers a service or facilities which require the community to come to it, it should do so in such a way that minimum effort is needed. We found that one way of doing this is to offer one service (an advice office) under the cover of another (a shop), which does not make people feel threatened. We set up a nearly-new clothes and coffee shop called "Street Level". It looked like an ordinary shop, so people felt confident about coming in, even though they knew it was run by the local church. The clothes and food were prepared, packaged and presented well so that there was no "cut-price" stigma attached to them. The environment in the shop was pleasant and relaxing: it was a place where people felt happy to talk.

Through the shop we were able to offer informal counselling, information and even a service for people who needed some help with filling in forms. I believe that if we had instead opened an office performing these functions, far fewer people would have come in.

Through "Street Level" many people have been helped and many new projects have been spawned. The lives of some of the people who have been contacted through it have subsequently been transformed by the love and power of God. One such person is Margaret Roulston. This is her story:

I was brought up in a religious background in Glasgow. My uncle Sam, who often visited my family, was a Salvation Army brigadier and had been a missionary in Africa. I was sent to the local Church of Scotland church every Sunday without fail. When I was about ten I began to look at religion in a strange way. I tried all sorts of religious sects, but I thought they were full of hypocrites. When I was twelve years old Uncle Sam tried to force me to become a Salvationist. I used to take part in the singing in the streets and pubs.

When I was fifteen years old I rebelled against my parents and my religion. It's not too easy to explain why, but I'll have a go. When I was very young I used to ask my parents if I was theirs. They would say I was. But when I was fifteen they told me that I was fostered. I didn't mind that. But when they told me that I had brothers and sisters, and that my real mother had abandoned us all in turn at the age of three, I felt deeply hurt. I even tried to kill myself.

I hated my real mother. I wanted to destroy her. Things at home got worse after that. Uncle Sam told me that being a good Christian meant forgiving my mother. But it wasn't that easy for me, because I blamed God. My step-parents told me that they had given me a good home and that I should be grateful.

I ran away to London when I was sixteen. I got into bad company, mixing with people who had no morals at all. I took to drink and soon became an alcoholic. I went on the game to support my drinking. I got caught by the police and was sent to Borstal for three years. I was twenty when I came out, and I went straight back to London and my old way of life.

I tried to stop drinking. I failed at first, but in the end I succeeded. I met Don when I was twenty-five and went to live with him. He didn't want me to stay on the game, so I went to work in a factory. There I made some friends for the first time in my life.

I got to know some members of All Saints Church at their nearly-new clothes shop, "Street Level". One day I met a young girl there who was a Christian. She invited me to go and see her get baptized at All Saints. I liked the service and the people. It made me stop and think about God. I started going to the services quite often. I was forty-one by this time.

At one service one of the church members happened to say to me and the friend I was with that he was sitting with two nice ladies. I began to cry, because I thought I was a really horrible person.

I had suffered with migraine all my life, and I was in pain with it that evening. God healed and delivered me from it there and then. I wanted to become a Christian, so I gave my heart to God that evening. I got baptized myself in the summer.

I often think about the fact that God loved us so much that He sent His Son, Jesus, to save us – to save me. Psalm 91 has been a great comfort to me. Here are the first four verses:

> He who dwells in the shelter of the Most High will rest in the shadow of the Almighty. I will say of the Lord, "He is my refuge and my fortress, my God, in whom I trust." Surely he will save you from the fowler's snare and from the deadly pestilence. He will cover you with his feathers, and under his wings you will find refuge; his faithfulness will be your shield and rampart.

2.5 Past and present

Understanding the community in which the church is set helps prevent false assumptions being made about people. Understanding the traditions and social history of an area provides vital clues to people's attitudes – including their attitude to the Christian Gospel. This is a fundamental approach in the missionary enterprise which we cannot bypass: understanding the culture which is so often locked into the history of the area.

Care needs to be taken in getting as clear a picture as possible of the overall situation in the community. It was for this reason that we spent a good proportion of our time in our first few months at All Saints auditing the community and the congregation. Ever since then understanding our community has been a continuous priority. Even after the original surveys and audits we have continued to seek to understand the area in which we live.

In those early months we were particularly interested to learn why the community was the way it was. We set a small team of people to work researching the area. It became clear that Brixton Prison, situated some 600 yards from the church, was the key to an understanding of the community. We found that in many ways the character of Brixton Hill had been shaped by the prison.

It was originally known as the Surrey House of Correction and was built in 1819–20 for female prisoners sentenced to hard labour. The prison soon became known as an unhealthy place, since over 400 inmates were crammed into a building originally designed to house just 175.

In the middle of the nineteenth century the prison was extended so as to accommodate 700–800 women, most of whom were uneducated single mothers who had been convicted for theft or prostitution. There was a convict nursery where children were kept up to the age of four. After that they were forced to leave, and presumably they became child slaves in the workhouses and factories. The children seldom saw any men except the chaplain and the surgeon. One male visitor once noted that the children were scared of him, since they weren't used to men.

The prison closed towards the end of the century and reopened in 1902 as a gaol for men. By this time Brixton and Brixton Hill had grown, and Brixton Hill in particular had developed around the prison, dominated both by the gaol's physical presence and by the human presence of so many prison officers and ex-convicts.

The Clapham Sect, a group of evangelical social reformers based at Holy Trinity Church, Clapham, planted the church called All Saints in response to the needs of this growing community. All Saints and the London City Mission – perhaps seeking to save children from slavery in the factories or from being sent up chimneys as sweeps – began two schools in the area. They were built near the precincts of the prison, and the school buildings, though largely derelict, can still be seen today. In addition All Saints also worked among the poor and needy right from the start. The records show that hundreds of blankets were lent to those who needed them, while shoes were provided for children, and food was given to the poor and the sick.

There would seem to be a connection between Brixton Hill's past history and its condition today. The community grew up around a women's prison, and in some ways it still operates like a women's prison today. Many single women with children move into council accommodation in the area. Once they are there it is very difficult for them to escape, since the council has very little alternative accommodation to offer them.

In 1989 forty-eight per cent of the children born in Lambeth were born in single-parent families. In Brixton Hill this per-

---

Historical research checklist

- Walk around the area and observe its characteristics today (noting the age and founder of older buildings such as churches, schools etc.).

- Find out when the main housing was built, note the size and quality of the majority of dwellings. Are residential areas well cared for or neglected?

- Discover the foundations of the community – look at old maps and local history books (you can usually find these in the local library). Visit the town hall.

- Speak to older members of the community about life as it used to be – they are an invaluable resource. Try to learn about key events in the history of the community (tragedies, victories, major upheavals, etc.).

- Study the local census figures (these will be in the local library).

- Concentrating on the information you have gathered, list the key problems in the community today as you see them, and pray for discernment, wisdom and guidance to tackle them.

centage is probably even higher. The census carried out a decade ago revealed that two-thirds of the community's people aged twenty-one or over were women, and this percentage is even higher now. Men are a rarity in many of the children's lives. They are often no more than "visitors" to the families which they have fathered. The children grow up with a poor image of men, and the boys have few good role models to emulate. As a result they in their turn grow up to become absentee fathers and husbands, like their own fathers were. The responsibilities of family life fall heavily upon the shoulders of the women and the older children, who have to grow up early to help their mothers take care of the younger ones. It is not surprising that the rates of infant mortality and child abuse are among the highest in the country.

Any local community will contain within its life factors such as these – they are the barriers which Satan builds to block the progress of the Kingdom of God. Prayerful observation and historical research can lead to the identification of those barriers. Through prayer and action they can then be brought down. All our work for God – indeed, our whole life – becomes spiritual warfare if we are aware of what it is that we are fighting and praying against. Direct demonic manifestations and specific deliverance should not be ruled out, but this ministry alone is not enough: we must also work to destroy Satan's power by prayer and action in the community.

2.6 Reflections on the theology of the Incarnation

God wants us to identify with those around us. As Paul put it, we should "Rejoice with those who rejoice" and "mourn with those who mourn" (Romans 12:15). To identify with others is to obey our highest calling, which is to be like Jesus. As it says in Philippians, we should not hang on to our status and position, but we should instead be like Jesus, who took on human flesh, became a servant and died for others (Philippians 2:5–11).

In Jesus God became flesh – He identified with us and lived with us. By this He demonstrated His love for us. He became a human being in order to complete the rescue plan that would save us and draw us back to Him.

When I was a young man studying at college I came home one day to find that my dad wanted me to do a particularly unpleasant job. He took me into the back garden and pointed at the kitchen drain. He said my long arms were needed to unblock it! I reluctantly got to work and reached down into the drain and removed the muck which had been blocking it. The stench was so terrible that I was almost sick.

It seems to me that Jesus' coming into the world as a man and living amongst us was something like the unpleasant task my dad asked me to do – except, of course, that what Jesus did was of infinitely greater importance. He gave up the glory of heaven and came into the world, with all its muck and filth. He was prepared to go to any lengths to identify with us and rescue us. We must imitate His example. If the Kingdom of God is to be seen, the Church which bears witness to that Kingdom must identify itself with the community.

In order for Jesus to reveal His Kingdom, He needed to be a King with us; even though He was with us, He was able to maintain His identity as King. In order for Jesus to reveal His Kingdom through us, we need to be with others but also to maintain our identity as subjects of the King.

For the Church to be effective in bringing the love of God to bear on people's lives it must live and identify with those it seeks to reach. There is nothing new in this: much of the New Testament is concerned with highlighting and explaining this idea. The problem for us is this: how do we identify with our communities so that the Kingdom is shown to be present in the world today?

Of course, there are risks attached to all this. If we are not careful, identification can lead to us losing our uniqueness as God's people, and can end with our distinctive witness being whittled away. The temptation to conform to the pattern of the society around us is a powerful one. Jesus was confronted with this temptation during His forty days and nights in the desert. He is able to sympathize with our difficulties in this area, because He too was "tempted in every way, just as we are – yet was without sin" (Hebrews 4:15).

In order to bring the Kingdom into the world Jesus had to take risks, and we too have to take risks if His Kingdom is to be revealed through us. But risky though it is, identification with the world around us is not just something for the radical fringe of the Church – rather, it is an imperative for the whole of the Church. It is clear that if we are to manifest the Kingdom and live as Jesus' disciples we must identify with those around us and live as their servants.

Identification involves risk and consumes our time, resources and energy. The other side of the coin is that identification leads to visibility within the community, access into other people's lives and opportunities to communicate the Gospel to people face-to-face.

The essential thing we must guard against is creating an image of ourselves as providers or benefactors. This is not the way of Christian discipleship and obedience.

> Jesus said to them, "The kings of the Gentiles lord it over them; and those that exercise authority over them call themselves benefactors. But you are not to be like that . . . you should be like the youngest . . . like one who serves" (Luke 22:25–26).

We are not benefactors who have only ourselves to offer. In fact, if we try to offer *our* resources, we often prevent God from offering *His*. God is our only true provider. It is clear that if we are to stay faithful to the Kingdom and live as disciples we must identify with those around us and regard ourselves as the servants of others.

Unfortunately the Church has fallen so far from genuine identification that it is now difficult to know where to begin. However, that should not prevent us from sincerely seeking to realize this goal.

Jesus said His disciples were to be salt and light in the world.

When salt is in food it is virtually invisible, and yet its effect is immediately recognizable. Light, on the other hand, in order to be effective, must be visible to everyone. The Church is called to identify with the community (that is, to be salt), but it is also called to present a public witness to Christ (that is, to be a light).

3

Planning

3.1 The importance of planning

We have already identified six elements in the Learning Loop – observation, review, discussion, planning, communication and action. In this chapter we are going to take a closer look at planning.

When a church is confronted by a community's needs the temptation is always to respond reactively and quickly without sufficient forethought and planning. We need to make plans on the basis of what we believe God has said, and we need to respond to the needs He has highlighted. In this chapter I would like to reveal some of the methods which we have employed in making a planned response to the needs of the community around us.

If we see planning as part of the practical outworking of our faith, then we will stop thinking of it as a rather dull optional extra which has little to do with our spiritual life, and begin to see it as something which is vitally important. If we regard planning as essential to the process of meeting the needs of the community, there will be less time wasted on discussion about its relevance.

Some Christians believe that planning is positively unspiritual and prevents God from doing what He wants to do! But this view is based on a fundamental misunderstanding. The sort of planning I am advocating is that which is done in the light of revelation from God. We need first to learn from Him the direction in which we should be going and what our goals should be. Then we need to make every effort to be obedient to His will and to work towards His goals by making plans that will get us from where we are to where He wants us to be.

3.2 Biblical precedents for planning

The Bible is full of advice about planning and examples of it. The book of Proverbs is a good place to start. We may ask ourselves, is it wise to think and plan ahead? "Sensible people always think before they act, but stupid people advertise their ignorance" (Proverbs 13:16, GNB). We may ask, what will planning do for us? "Sensible people will see trouble coming and avoid it, but an unthinking person will walk right into it and regret it later" (22:3). We may ask, is it right to know what to do in the future? "Why is a clever person wise? Because he knows what to do. Why is a stupid person foolish? Because he only thinks he knows" (14:8). "A fool will believe anything; sensible people watch their step" (14:15).

Even though Proverbs seems so clear about the need to plan ahead, we may still wonder whether Jesus, who has ushered in the new era of the Spirit, wants us to make plans. But to me it seems clear that Jesus Himself made plans, both for Himself and for His disciples:

- Jesus knew the purpose of His mission and was able to plan on the basis of that knowledge. On one occasion He said to His disciples, "'Let us go somewhere else – to the nearby villages – so I can preach there also. That is why I have come.' So He travelled throughout Galilee, preaching in their synagogues and driving out demons" (Mark 1:38–39).

- Jesus understood His mission in detail and so made detailed plans. "As the time approached for Him to be taken up to heaven, Jesus resolutely set out for Jerusalem, and He sent messengers on ahead. They went into a Samaritan village to get things ready for Him" (Luke 9:51–52).

- Jesus revealed the mission of the Church to His disciples and gave them a basic strategy for achieving it: "Therefore go and make disciples of all nations, baptizing them in the name of the

Father and of the Son and of the Holy Spirit, and teaching them to obey everything I have commanded you. And surely I will be with you always, to the very end of the age" (Matthew 28:19–20).

- Jesus also gave His disciples more detailed plans for implementing the overall strategy: "But you will receive power when the Holy Spirit comes on you; and you will be my witnesses in Jerusalem, and in all Judea and Samaria, and to the ends of the earth" (Acts 1:8).

Also, it is clear from other parts of Scripture that God has from the beginning planned salvation:

- "In Him we were also chosen, having been predestined according to the plan of Him who works out everything in conformity with the purpose of His will" (Ephesians 1:11).

- "You see, just at the right time, when we were still powerless, Christ died for the ungodly" (Romans 5:6).

In addition, the Bible contains the stories of many great projects which were accomplished through human agents, and which could not have been achieved without careful planning in response to God's revealed will. For example:

- The Exodus under Moses.
- The conquest of the Promised Land under Joshua.
- The building of the Temple under Solomon.
- The rebuilding of the walls of Jerusalem under Nehemiah.
- The mission to the Gentiles under Paul.

All of these projects were born through revelation from God, and all the individuals involved in them were called by God, but there was also planning every step of the way.

Once a plan was made – whether it was Jesus' plan to go to Jerusalem or Nehemiah's plan to build the wall or Moses' plan to lead the people to the Promised Land – it had to be communicated to others and acted upon. Some of the leaders in biblical times were not good communicators – Moses, for example – but each of them had to find a way of communicating with others and drawing them into the divine plan. For example, Nehemiah told his people, "You see the trouble we are in: Jerusalem lies in ruins, and its gates have been burned with fire. Come, let us rebuild the wall of Jerusalem, and we will no longer be in disgrace" (Nehemiah 2:17). He drew the community into his plan so that it could be shared, implemented and completed. No matter how good a plan is, it will stand or fall according to how well it is communicated and how much others are encouraged to take it on board as their own.

A clear and well-presented plan gives people the opportunity to give their committed support, or to withhold it. When undertaking any new adventure of faith, it is essential to know who is going to be behind it all the way and to ensure sufficient resources to carry it through.

Taking a risk and failing is not necessarily a bad thing when we have given it our best shot, but ill-conceived projects which are begun with great enthusiasm and then abandoned because difficulties were not anticipated are discouraging to everyone, and do not bring glory to our faithful God.

3.3   Good planning and bad planning

Any plan must take account of the needs which have to be met, the obstacles which have to be overcome and the total situation in which the plan is to operate.

Bad planning concentrates more on tomorrow than on next year. Good planning concentrates on the overall direction of the project and seeks to include details which support its overall purpose.

Bad Planning

Tomorrow   Next week   Next month   Next year →

Good Planning

What needs to be done tomorrow/ this week	Medium- term objectives	Longer- term objectives	Overall direction/ purpose

Often we expend so much energy in reacting to the problems of today and tomorrow that we have little left for working at long-term goals. Because of this many of the needs in our communities, to which the Church could and should respond, are never considered, let alone met. God has little opportunity to demonstrate creatively His love and concern for the world if His people are doing no more than reacting to immediate problems and situations.

It can be seen from the above diagram that if time and energy are spent on describing the overall purpose and aims of a project, the short-term objectives and the things that need to be done today are easier to plan.

It is important that we should write down the goals and aims at each stage, and that what is written should be measurable and specific. For example, when stating the overall purpose of the project we should resist the temptation to use vague slogans like "bringing in the Kingdom" or battle-cries like "evangelize the lost".

4

First Things First: Worship

If a church is to grow, then getting its worship right is not an option but the number one priority. This should be not a half-hearted enterprise but a whole-hearted one. Whether we are familiar with more traditional styles of worship or more contemporary ones is not the issue – what matters is our desire to meet with God and to hear from Him. Together with prayer, worship is the motor which drives a church along, and as such it should be given the central place which it deserves.

4.1 "In-drag"

I have found that two different approaches to evangelism are needed. In one people come to us and in the other we go to them. The first is what I call "in-drag" and the second is outreach. In this chapter we will be dealing with in-drag, and we will cover outreach in Chapter 6.

For the most part in British churches, evangelistic methods have depended upon in-drag. The Church of England is particularly good at this approach, and has fostered links in a relatively friendly environment with a broad fringe of uncommitted and nominal "Christians". This fringe has been the main target of evangelism, and the objective has been to bring these people into committed membership. One of the main ways of reaching the fringe has been "the occasional offices" – baptisms, marriages and funerals (affectionately referred to as the "hatch, match and despatch" ministry). Many people start coming to regular Sunday services as a result of contact with the Church at these important times in their lives.

In order for a church to have any confidence in reaching and teaching those who come to it via in-drag, two priorities must be addressed: (a) the organization of services to enable the people to meet with God in worship, and (b) the organization of services to ensure effective communication of the Gospel. Generally speaking, (a) tends to be more theological and (b) more practical. Both of these priorities are vital to the effectiveness of a church's life.

All Saints has tried to make the most of the opportunities which in-drag presents. People who come to church under their own steam, for whatever reason, should have the opportunity to hear and to respond to the Gospel. Not only the sermon but the whole service should communicate God's love. Often we hear that visitors who have come to one of our services have been deeply affected by it.

4.2   The Family Service

We try to ensure that the whole of the weekly Family Service (11.30 a.m.) is a medium of communication. We use an overhead projector not only for the songs but also to illustrate the talk. We have found that if this is handled in the right manner, it need not be just a children's talk – rather, it can be an illustrated talk for every age. If you have a talk which is strictly for children, often the children feel talked down to and the adults are excluded. But if a straight-forward and direct message is prepared – one which both illuminates the biblical text and applies it to people's lives – then all ages can be taught at the same time.

During the time of prayer we often split into groups. We ask people to turn to those next to them and to form groups of between four and six. We encourage the people in the groups to pray for one another and for important issues, and to listen to what God is saying to them. Then there is an opportunity for people to share with the rest of the congregation whatever they have heard from God – people often share pictures and visions, lines from choruses and hymns which have spoken to them, personal stories and insights, and particularly verses from Scripture. To ensure that what is shared is heard and communicated effectively, we ask people to "stand up, speak up and shut up"! All of this has a powerful effect on visitors.

By the time we have the sermon or talk, those present have already heard from God in various ways, and many illustrations and examples of His purpose, presence and power have been given. So the person who gives the talk often finds that he or she has a very receptive audience. Even so, in our talks we try to use two or three of the following communication media:

- *Verbal illustrations:* true stories, newspaper cuttings, quotations, personal testimonies and everyday activities.
- *Visual illustrations:* usually on the overhead projector.
- *Three-dimensional illustrations:* drama, interviews, props to illustrate a point.

Through the use of varied illustrations the message is approached from a number of different directions, and so those who hear it have a better chance of taking away and remembering what they have heard.

People generally remember at most 20 per cent of what they *hear*, but 40 per cent of what they *hear and see*, and 60 per cent of what they *hear, see and do*. So it is also important to involve people in doing things in the services. There is a high level of participation in the leading and running of them. Members of the congregation take part in a number of different ways. Responsibility for preaching is shared by a team. People are often deeply affected by what they do in a service.

4.3   The Traditional Service

The Traditional Service (10.00 a.m.) is based on the Morning Prayer format in the Alternative Service Book, and is intended for those who prefer a more conventional style of worship. The service, though liturgical, is simple. Hymns are sung and a

---

Family Service checklist

- Keep the structure of the service simple.

- Keep the language straightforward.

- Ensure that the jobs which can be delegated are delegated (e.g. reading, praying, worship, welcoming people at the door).

- Hold a short pre-service briefing to ensure that all those who will be participating know what they are supposed to be doing.

- Ensure that all those participating will pray for the service beforehand.

- Ensure that those with especially significant roles have an opportunity after the service to review their part in it.

---

standard sermon is preached. We do not use visual illustrations, but we do try to keep the sermon uncomplicated and direct. Verbal illustrations are used often, and the sermon is not more than fifteen minutes long. I lead and preach in a third of the services, while the leadership team are responsible for the other services. The Bible readings and prayers are done by members of the congregation. Although the service is formal, there is room for some spontaneity, and those who lead the worship and prayers are encouraged to share anything they have learned from God that week.

We know that those who are drawn to this type of service are also those who expect the local church to exercise a traditional pattern of ministry, and this includes visiting, which they appreciate. So the team responsible for running this service is developing a ministry of visiting within the parish. However, we depart from tradition in one respect: instead of the vicar visiting everyone, this work is now done by a team.

4.4 The Informal Service

The Informal Service (7.00 p.m.) is orientated towards those who prefer a more relaxed approach to worship. Music plays a central role in the service, and we have a "band" of up to six musicians and three singers. Many of the songs used are contemporary worship songs, but almost all of them have been adapted by the worship team, using such styles as soul, gospel, house, reggae, rap and ska – all of which reflect the rich cultural variety of our parish. As well as using material written by others, the worship team also write their own worship songs.

The talk may rely to some extent on visual aids, but is usually presented in a narrative style. Sometimes this means that it may last for as long as half an hour, but the congregation, largely made up of teenagers and young adults, seems to find this "laid-back" approach helpful.

We usually allow time for people to respond to the talk and apply the message. The congregation splits into groups to discuss and pray over what they have heard. This means that there is participation in the learning process, which is often further augmented by individuals sharing what God has been saying to them during the worship.

As with the others, the responsibility for leading and organizing these services is in the hands of the congregational team. Again, I am responsible for a third of the services while the rest of the team handles the other two-thirds.

Each of our three services has developed over a period of time into a fully fledged congregation with its own style, ministry and vision.

4.5   Worship – the top priority

At All Saints worship is our number one priority. We have found that as we express our love for God in worship and prayer, others who may not know Him are drawn in. Worship itself can communicate the Gospel effectively. It is not unusual for visitors to comment on the quality and sincerity of the worship. Many, even non-Christians, say they have met with God in a real and personal way through it. On occasion visitors have run out of a service in tears because they have had an awesome encounter with God.

Our approach to worship is based on an appreciation of both Scripture and experience. It is quite clear from even the most shallow reading of Scripture that worship of God should be the first priority of all His people. The Old Testament is saturated with references to worship, both corporate and individual. Jesus Himself made it clear that God the Father actually seeks worshippers, particularly worshippers who come to Him in spirit and in truth (John 4:23–24). The Devil tried to get Jesus to worship him, realizing that in this single act Jesus would forfeit His Kingdom and destroy His own destiny (Luke 4:5–8). The vision of heaven in the Book of Revelation describes an environment where worship is a constant reality.

In Chapter 1 I wrote about the burns I received as a result of an accident with some petrol. I had to spend some time in hospital after this, and through this period of convalescence worship became the central focus of my life. I spent many hundreds of hours studying the subject of worship in Scripture, and probably as many hours learning about worship through doing it – by myself and with others. As we learned to enter into an intimate experience of worship, so the evidence of God's presence increased. Teaching, healing, deliverance, evangelism and reconciliation between people were now by-products of worship. Just as I have personally discovered worship, so has All Saints as a whole.

In the early months of my time at All Saints, the informal evening service saw many remarkable events. Sometimes the services would last for as long as three or four hours. Much of this time was spent in worship. As we learned to listen to God and to share what we heard, so we integrated what we had discovered into the pattern of the church's life. As we learned about healing, so we made time to practise on one another. As we realized God's desire for heartfelt worship, so we spent longer periods simply seeking to give Him pleasure by worshipping Him. As I look back, I am sure that these extended times of worship in the evening services were necessary in order for us to learn some of the important truths which were later to impact upon the whole church and upon the wider community.

Before I got to All Saints I had already begun to reflect upon the subject of corporate worship, and my experience at All Saints has filled out those early reflections. What follows is a description of worship as I understand it. It is not intended to be a prescription for every church; it is simply an account of what I have experienced.

4.6 The Corporate Worship Curve

In Scripture worship is often associated with climbing a hill or mountain, sometimes literally and sometimes metaphorically. Most of the centres of Israelite worship were sited on high places – the Temple Mount in Jerusalem is the prime example. Many of the significant events in the Bible happened on hills or mountains – take, for instance, God's covenant with Noah on Ararat, Abraham offering Isaac as a sacrifice, Moses receiving the Law, Solomon building the Temple, Jesus' sermon on the Mount and His transfiguration, crucifixion and ascension.

"Going up" to worship the Lord was an actual physical experience for the Israelite on his way to the Temple. Thus it became part of familiar biblical symbolism and was even used when the place of worship became less significant, as it did during the exile and later, with the development of the synagogues. Even today pilgrimages to Temple Mount have a great significance for the Jewish believer.

For the Christian, "going up" to worship is more to do with an attitude of heart. Jesus made it clear that the actual place of worship was no longer important: "Believe me," He said to the Samaritan woman, "a time is coming when you will worship the Father neither on this mountain nor in Jerusalem . . . a time is coming and has now come when the true worshippers will worship the Father in spirit and truth, for they are the kind of worshippers the Father seeks" (John 4:21, 23). However, in the New Testament the idea of "going up" to worship still remains in a symbolic sense. The writer of the letter to the Hebrews compares the old covenant with the new in these words: "You have not come to a mountain that can be touched and that is burning with fire; to darkness, gloom and storm [i.e. Mount Sinai, symbolizing the old covenant] . . . But you have come to Mount Zion, to the heavenly Jerusalem, the city of the living God. You have come to thousands upon thousands of angels in joyful assembly, to the church of the firstborn, whose names are written in heaven. You have come to God, the judge of all men, to the spirits of righteous men made perfect, to Jesus the mediator of a new covenant" (Hebrews 12:18, 22–24). So coming to God to worship Him is still spoken of in terms of going up a mountain. In Revelation 14:1 there is a similar picture of the Church gathered on Mount Zion, in the new Jerusalem.

Reflecting on all this has led me to understand and to teach worship in terms of the mountain symbol. So as to communicate this concept as clearly as possible I have developed it into what I call the Corporate Worship Curve. Again, I would emphasize that what follows is not a fixed prescription for the way in which worship should be understood, planned and carried out; rather, it is a description of how I and those working with me have entered into worship. I offer the Worship Curve simply as a method of communicating the key elements of worship. It is drawn as a graph on two axes – time spent with God in worship

The Corporate Worship Curve

Intimacy with God

Stage 5: Commission
 The worshippers go out into
 the world, empowered by
 the Spirit.
 God commissions His
 people.

Stage 4: Consummation
 The worshippers receive
 and express the gifts of
 the Spirit and the blessing
 of God's presence.
 God reveals Himself in
 word and deed.

Stage 3: Adoration

 The worshippers
 draw near to God.
 God pours out His Spirit.

Stage 2: Reflection

 The worshippers
 confess their sins.
 God forgives their sins.

Stage 1: Exaltation

 The worshippers praise God.
 God receives praise from His
 people and welcomes them.

Time

and intimacy with God. (Obviously, this is not a "real" graph, as intimacy with God cannot really be measured.)

Stage 1: Exaltation

Praise and thanksgiving should mark the beginning of worship. Psalm 100:4 says, "Enter His gates with thanksgiving and His courts with praise."

In the Old Testament there are a number of different words associated with worship. *Zamar* means the joyful expression of praise through musical instruments (Psalm 150:3f.), and *halal* means making a loud noise. Both of these elements of worship are more appropriate to this stage than to any of the others. The volume and pace of the music and songs are important at this stage, as they should express the joy with which the believers are entering into corporate worship.

Stage 2: Reflection

From praising God simply for the fact that He is God, we move on to reflecting upon His nature and attributes: He is all-knowing, all-powerful, eternal, loving, merciful and righteous.

Readings from Scripture are an effective way of focusing the worshippers' attention upon God at this stage. Coming to an awareness of who God is leads us to repentance, and so corporate confession of sin is often appropriate at this stage. It may be helpful to have a sermon now, since this will further concentrate the minds of the worshippers.

Stage 3: Adoration

Through a recognition of the attributes of God we are moved to adore Him. As we adore Him and open ourselves to His presence, so He anoints and fills us with His Spirit. The exercise and administration of the gifts of the Spirit is therefore often appropriate at this stage.

Stage 4: Consummation

Awe draws us still closer to God, so that we desire to meet with

Him in a profound, "face-to-face" encounter. This is always life-changing.

The gifts which God pours out upon us are for the encouragement and upbuilding of the whole church. As the gifts are exercized we become aware of God meeting our needs. His wisdom and knowledge change the direction of our lives and His healing and deliverance lead us towards greater wholeness. All of this brings a strong sense of God's personal presence amongst the body of believers worshipping together.

It may be appropriate at this stage for a sermon to be preached, as this can lead on to the next stage.

Stage 5: Commission

Once we have encountered God, He always sends us out with thanksgiving to reach His world with His love. As we leave church after a time of worship we should be prepared to leave the mountains of God's presence and enter the valleys of the world. As Jesus, Peter, James and John came down from the mount of transfiguration they encountered a demonized epileptic child who needed healing. As we are sent forth by God into the world, we should expect to be confronted with needs which must be met in the power of His Spirit.

The Worship Curve and music

The music used in a service can be organized to flow along the line of the Worship Curve. The songs and hymns can be arranged into five groups. Here is a sample selection arranged in this fashion:

Stage 1: Exaltation: Hosanna
                      Praise Him on the Trumpet
                      Thine Be the Glory
Stage 2: Reflection: You Laid Aside Your Majesty
                      Ascribe Greatness
                      Amazing Grace

Stage 3: Adoration: I love You, Lord
                         Jesus, Take Me As I Am
                         Breathe on Me, Breath of God
Stage 4: Consummation: You Are Beautiful Beyond Description
                         For Thou, O Lord
                         My God, How Wonderful Thou Art
Stage 5: Commission: Shine, Jesus, Shine
                         In Heavenly Armour
                         Guide Me, O Thou Great Jehovah

Some of the songs can be used at more than one stage, depending on the emphasis used by the worship leader. For example, songs used at Stage 1 can often be used at Stage 5 as well.

Tempo is important at each stage. Generally the tempo slows between Stage 1 and Stage 4, as the songs become more thoughtful, personal and reflective. The tempo quickens again at Stage 5, as the people get ready to go out into the world.

We have found that our concept of the Worship Curve, though it might appear to reduce leading worship to a technique, has been extremely helpful to those just starting out in worship leading. It provides a ready-made framework for any occasion, and allows worship leaders to order the material they select.

4.7   Worship and the power of God

Worship is an environment in which we can expect God to act powerfully and speak prophetically through the body of Christ. At All Saints we have seen this happen many times. One person who has been touched by the power of God through worship is Beccy Cripps, who is now a full-time youth worker at the church.

Beccy had come to the church to help us with our summer playscheme. We had heard that she had a disease in her left arm, but none of us had realized how serious it was. When she arrived she was wearing a metal brace on her arm. She told us that the blood supply to the bones in the arm was restricted and that effectively the arm was dying. She had already had prayer for it, and as a result she was experiencing less pain than before, but the disease was still present and was growing in its effect. Privately I doubted whether she would be able to manage as a playscheme worker.

The night before the playscheme was to begin Beccy came to our evening service. I was teaching on the healing ministry of Jesus. During the service three individuals, at separate times, said they believed there was someone in the service with a debilitating problem in their left arm. With some trepidation a small team of people under my direction began to pray for Beccy and for two others with different problems, whilst I talked the congregation through the process. As my wife, Sally, began to pray for her, Beccy fell over under the power of the Holy Spirit. Sally and the prayer team continued to pray for her. Although she was still conscious, she was unable to move.

Although she seemed to feel better there and then, it wasn't until the next day that Beccy felt the full effects of what had happened. She had been unable to use her arm normally for almost two years. Simple tasks like washing her hair or washing up had been impossible. Without realizing the significance of what she was doing, she washed her breakfast dishes that morning! For some reason it wasn't until she was playing basketball that afternoon that she realized that she had been fully healed. Her arm even looked different. It was no longer thin and wasted as it had been, but was now strong and healthy, just like her other arm. It was covered with muscle tissue which had not been there the day before.

When she went home after the playscheme was finished her healing had a remarkable effect upon her family and friends. Some of her Christian friends really grew in their faith, and some of the others actually committed themselves to Jesus because of what He had done for her. Two of the doctors who had been treating her were very positive about what had happened and were open to the idea that she may have been healed by God, but the others simply concluded that the original diagnosis must have been wrong.

For Beccy the experience has not only been a personal encouragement but has also been an opportunity to reach out to others with the Good News of Christ. Her story is a clear example of something happening in a service affecting the outside world.

Julie Connell is another person whose life was touched by the power of God at one of the services at All Saints. This is her story:

It was the birth of my son, Rupert, which brought the issue to a head. It seemed important to me to bring him up in the Christian faith, but I felt inadequate. My husband and I put off getting him christened. I thought about the confirmation vows which I had taken years ago. I was afraid to repeat them on behalf of my son. My faith was too weak, and I did not want to compromise myself again. For months I turned the problem over in my head. My conscience would not let the matter rest. Then, almost seventeen months after Rupert was born, I finally plucked up enough courage to set foot inside All Saints Church.

It is only just around the corner from where I live, and yet this was a giant step for me. I was not prepared for the impact which this visit would make on me. I knew at once that there were genuine believers in the congregation. The sermon was powerful, and it struck at my heart in two ways. Hearing the story of Paul's dramatic conversion on the road to Damascus stirred up my old feelings of resentment. Why hadn't anything like that ever happened to me? Also in the sermon was a wonderful illustration of how Jesus suffers for us when we suffer. This left me wondering why I could possibly want to turn my back on Him. I could sense His presence in the church. It was beautiful. I was deeply shaken. The church had laid down a challenge. My instinctive reaction was to run away from it.

I discussed my feelings with my husband, and he realized

that I needed his help. He didn't know what to expect, but he went to the church on my behalf two weeks later, even though he wasn't a Christian himself. He introduced himself to the vicar, Mike Breen. After that Mike began calling on us to tell us about the Christian faith.

The first time he called I told him that my beliefs went only so far – I felt that I didn't have a personal relationship with God. When he asked me how I felt about that I broke into tears. As the weeks went by I felt increasingly excited and yet apprehensive at the same time. I felt that my husband and I were being drawn on in faith, and my resistance lessened all the time. At one service Mike spoke about the crucifixion, and I understood its significance for the first time in my life.

With hindsight I can see how important it was that Mike prayed with us specific prayers for us. Nobody had ever done that for us before. One evening he told us he knew we had received the gift of the Holy Spirit. As time passed we knew for ourselves that this was true.

We fixed a date for the christening: 18th December. The focal point for me was the baptismal vows. Would I at some future time feel I had let God down again, having made those vows? Had I sought the Lord with all my heart this time?

The following week I decided I would take Communion again. I went along to the Midnight Communion on Christmas Eve full of expectancy. As we waited to take the bread and wine, Mike said we could take Communion if we knew the Lord. Now I had to take a decisive step of faith. I knew God's love, but did I know Him as a person? I decided to go forward, and as I returned to my seat afterwards to pray, I knew that the heavens had opened and were letting me in.

5

A New Approach to Youth Work

Driving home, my mind was full of all that I had seen and heard. I had just spent some days speaking at the Shaftesbury Society Annual Conference. A number of people had encouraged me to believe that God was going to do remarkable things at Brixton. Thinking through the implications of what some had shared made me overflow with excitement. Suddenly I was aware of God saying something: "What are you prepared to pay?" I wasn't sure what this meant. Did God mean that His gifts were not free? Did He mean that the fulfilment of the promises that I had heard had to be paid for? What was God trying to say? As I continued to pray and listen, I sensed God impressing upon me the cost of seeing His plans fulfilled, and I felt afraid. Six months previously my name had been all over the front pages of the South London newspapers, as "the vicar who kicks out kids". The church council had taken the decision to ask a private day nursery to leave the church premises, and my name was the one which was held up for scorn by the press. The huge misunderstandings, opposition, threats, scandal and lies which followed left me unwilling ever to go that way again, but I sensed that it was specifically this cost that God was highlighting: the cost of losing personal credibility in the eyes of the local community.

It seemed an impossible price, but by the time I arrived home I had admitted my fear and asked God to forgive my unwillingness. I prayed that God would give me courage to follow Him, even if it meant paying such a high price.

Within twenty-four hours of returning, two members of the church had been accused of immorality, and one, a trusted colleague, was accused of sexually assaulting young boys in the congregation. No preparation could have minimized the pain or shock at what had happened. Going through those first painful days and weeks, I again had to come to terms with the fact that, if the "story" got out, the local community would jump to all sorts of conclusions. The integrity of the church itself would be put in doubt. With the usual exaggeration which accompanies such accusations, none of us would be able to escape being tarnished. I dreaded the thought.

How would it be if the local community withdrew all good will towards us, if our uncommitted people stopped coming on Sundays, if parents stopped allowing their children to be involved in the youth project, and friendliness towards us was replaced by hostility? How would we exist, never mind grow, in such an environment? As I thought and prayed, I remembered that the Early Church often had to operate in a hostile environment. Far from retrenchment or decline, the Church in those early days actually grew to become the most important and powerful spiritual force in the Roman Empire. Also, I remembered the reports coming from mainland China, which were telling of the persecuted Church. After the missionaries had left it had gone through extreme persecution at the hands of the communist revolutionaries, and yet it had grown from around one million to something like sixty million. How could the Early Church, and the present-day persecuted Church, still grow in such hostile environments? I began to understand what God wanted me to learn.

I had to find out how the church could be maintained, and grow, despite hostility. I needed to learn these secrets. The survival and growth methods of the New Testament Church were easier to study than those of the persecuted Church because they were so clearly laid out and documented. I decided to study every example of mission strategy I could find in the New Testament, particularly concentrating on any account which revealed the achievements as well as the strategy. To my surprise I found that the methods adopted in the New Testament, particularly those of Jesus and His disciples, were similar to what we had been doing in our youth work for some time. Our youth work method was the practical outworking of a theology which we discovered afterwards! At first sight this may seem the wrong way around; you would expect to learn the theory before the practice. If, however, you look at the way Jesus taught and trained His disciples you see something quite different. Jesus used a "show and tell" method: first He would do something, then His disciples would do it. As I considered what God was revealing I began to understand that He had shown us the "how" and the "what" before He had explained the "why".

5.1   A-Teams
In general club-based youth work is on the decline, and this development seems to be a permanent one. Perhaps this is because the needs of young people have changed – their tastes in leisure have become more sophisticated. At the same time, family and community life, especially in the inner cities, has broken down, leaving young people alienated from institutional community facilities such as youth clubs. At one time parents and schools readily supported youth clubs and endorsed their work. Now this is less often the case, and even where it is the case young people are liable to rebel against officially endorsed youth activities.

So the widespread decline of youth clubs was one of the reasons why, when I was working as Team Leader at the Romsey Mill, the team and I decided to close the youth clubs we had been running and try something else. We would organize our youth work entirely around small, autonomous groups. Also, the team and I had been influenced by our reading about the Christian Base Communities of South America and their equivalents in the West. I think it was this that made us think about adopting a new approach to youth work.

We rejected club-based youth work not only because of the

decline of its popularity and effectiveness but also because of the unhelpful "provider-client" relationships which it created. The responsibility for the club programme was entirely in the hands of the youth worker running it, who would set up a club only to find that the one role available to him or her was that of a policeman, controlling the group and protecting the church buildings.

Also, we found that the dynamics of youth clubs could be a problem. Often they were dominated by a group of older boys who would intimidate the girls and the younger boys. This small group would end up monopolizing the space and equipment. The girls would be left to watch as the older boys played football; the younger boys would get a look-in if they were lucky! A youth worker running a club always had to struggle against these cliques, which made it difficult for new members to become integrated into the club.

- *Stop:* We had to abandon the old methods of youth work before the new methods could be tried.

- *Look:* We had to look carefully at the situation and make detailed plans for the future.

- *Listen:* We had to listen to the young people we worked with. We particularly had to listen to those who didn't come to the youth clubs and find out why they didn't come.

We spent six months planning our new approach to youth work. We involved the local secondary school and a large number of young people. We were convinced of the rightness of the change, and threw all our efforts into making the new groups work. Admittedly, when the time finally came to wind up the youth clubs, we felt sad about it and somewhat uncertain about the step we were taking. But the new approach turned out to be highly successful, and soon the new groups had three times more members than the old clubs had had. We had expected positive results, but even we were surprised by the scale of the success of the new approach.

I continued the work in Cambridge, where we called the small groups Alpha Groups. At All Saints we call them A-teams. In the A-teams we seek to enable the young people to grow to maturity in every way – socially, physically, mentally, emotionally and spiritually. The groups are based on the fact that young people need to belong. They need to feel secure in relationships where they are accepted, and they need to have the opportunity to commit themselves to something, knowing that others are committed to them.

Most young people tend to operate in small groups and gangs. These groups can be cliquey, but if they are given productive programmes and activities they can in fact make a positive contribution to young people's development towards adulthood. Small groups can provide a platform from which they can look towards the future. So in our A-teams project we are building upon a natural tendency among young people.

Small groups operate in every part of life, and in one way or another provide cohesion for society. Obviously the most basic group is the family, but where this is being broken down, other groups need to take over its role. At All Saints we have a strong emphasis on supporting and equipping families, but we also recognize that in today's society other social groups are necessary too.

5.2   How A-Teams work

An A-Team usually begins when a youth worker identifies a basic group of young people – a peer group or a group with a common interest. One can identify a group by asking one young person who his friends are and what he and they do together. The youth worker discusses with the young person the idea of starting a group which creates its own programme. He draws a simple spider-like diagram, with the young person in the middle and his friends all around him.

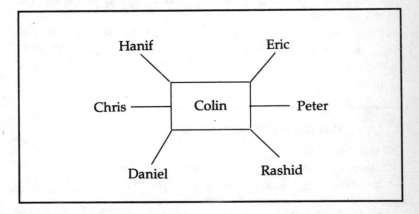

The youth worker then asks the young person to ask his friends if they are interested in starting such a group. Thus, from the outset, responsibility for the life and purpose of the group is put into the hands of its members.

At the group's first meeting the youth worker, who brings along an assistant, encourages the members to "brainstorm". All their ideas about what the group could do are written down, and then they are helped to select the six ideas which are to become the first six-week programme for the new A-Team.

The A-Teams at All Saints are usually single-sex, have between six and ten members and are very close-knit. They create progammes which cost little and contain both home-based activities (e.g. watching a video) and area-based ones (e.g. going swimming). Although all the groups are allowed to have whoever they want as members, all of them are multi-racial. The age range of the members is eight to sixteen years.

Each group has two youth workers assigned to it (i.e. the original youth worker and his or her assistant). They are the sort of people who are able quickly to develop relationships which are of the friend-to-friend type rather than the "provider-client" type. Their role is to offer ideas and organization while leaving the responsibility for the continuation of the group with the young people.

In this context all sorts of positive things take place. The size of the groups makes it easier for the members to develop their personalities and to learn social and relationship skills. There are

---

Making a six-week programme

Ideas:
Canoeing, abseiling, go-karting, swimming, skateboarding, weight-training, night hiking, assault courses, ten-pin bowling, basketball, self-defence, making a video, table tennis, ice-skating, roller-skating, going to the cinema, watching a video.

Programme (Tuesdays, 6.00–8.00 p.m.):

12th March	Planning
19th March	Swimming
26th March	Make a video
2nd April	Ten-pin bowling
9th April	Go-karting
16th April	Abseiling
23rd April	Going to the cinema

opportunities for them to share their difficulties and resolve their personal problems. Issues such as the misuse of drugs, violence in the home, sex and broken relationships can be dealt with in a practical way and not just at a theoretical level. Some of the young people who see themselves as failures at school or at home find that they can achieve personal success in an A-Team.

The youth worker's assistant is trained in leadership through observation and practice within the group. Eventually the assistant takes over from the youth worker, who moves on to start another A-Team. The new leader is then joined by an assistant of his own. So there is ample opportunity for the expansion of the whole programme. We augment the training process with special leaders' meetings, but most of the learning goes on face-to-face with young people.

The smallness of the groups makes leading them less stressful. A new youth worker finds that he has to deal not with a large youth club but with a small groups of friends.

Because the work is not based in a building but in the community, leaders are often able to visit the young people's homes at an early stage. Also the young people visit the leaders in their homes, quickly seeing them as friends.

Growing the Smaller Church

The growth and development of an A-Team

1 Two Workers find one
   person prepared to talk and
   listen

2 Two workers introduced to
   that person's peer group

3 Group begins to "gel" and
   talks about possible
   programme Initial 6-week
   programme agreed

4 Group active, planning
   running programme and
   reviewing progress

   While programme is
   running, group able to
   discuss and "live through"
   real life situations. Highs,
   lows, problems, and hassles
   talked through.

5 Leaders and workers give
   time to talk to individuals.

6 Some in groups show
   interest in Christian faith of
   workers.

7   Workers offer a short time
after or before A-Team to talk
things through about
Christian discipleship at
greater length

Some may become
Christians and are included
in the wider life of the church
whilst maintaining their
membership and
invovlement with the group

8   Possibly one leader leaves
group to help set up another
and a new leader comes. This
does not usually cause
instability in the group if it is
ensured that one worker is
left to continue and the new
worker is sensitive to pick up
where the other left off.

Occasionally, groups join
together for special events to
form secondary level group.

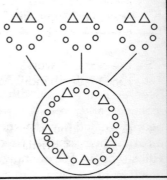

As the A-Teams project continues we are constantly discovering new positive aspects to the work. One of the greatest strengths of the system is the ease with which the team leaders can share their faith with the members. They are able to do this in a credible way which relates to the real experiences of the young people as they grow towards maturity. We have seen individual young people and even whole A-Teams come to faith in Christ. Sometimes worship, prayer and Bible study have then become part of a team's regular programme, and the members have become fully involved in the church.

A-Teams checklist

- Contact young people (mostly through schools).

- Identify a responsive invividual.

- Meet his/her peer group.

- Introduce the A-Team concept.

- Brainstorm ideas.

- Plan a six-week programme.

- Make friendships.

- Review progress and make another programme.

5.3   A-Teams and schools

Every A-Team begins with someone meeting a young person. We realized early on that if we were to make contact with young people we had to go to where they were. Obviously, they spend most of their time at school, so we built up links with Brixton Hill's schools. We are now welcomed in most of them, and as a result we have access to a large number of young people. The more we contact, the more we are able to network into our A-Teams.

People from All Saints now teach subjects such as music and games at all four of the local secondary schools. At present we are teaching American football and baseball. These games are currently very popular among the young people of our area, and we are the only local group prepared and able to teach them. These curricular lessons are augmented by informal and after-school activities which enable us to form A-Teams and so establish an "out-of-school" programme.

In our assemblies and lunchtime meetings we try to communicate to large groups of young people in a credible way. Sometimes we use a "roadshow" style of presentation, including music, visuals, drama and games, all based around a unifying theme.

This work with schools has been a major area of involvement for All Saints. We have been very encouraged as we have seen

---

Schools checklist

- Adopt a school.

- Begin to pray for the staff and pupils.

- Build relationships with the headteacher and his/her staff.

- Try to get church members on to the board of governors or the PTA. Ask to help with the assemblies.

- Gain access to curriculum time through subjects like RE, music, games, etc.

- Set up after-school groups, leading to involvement in A-Teams.

more and more doors open. Many hours of talking with
headteachers and other professionals have created a trusting
partnership between us and them. The schools project is proving
to be very beneficial not only for the young people but also for the
church members who are involved in it.

5.4   The A-Team concept applied to adults

We had always suspected that the A-Team concept was
transferable into work among adults, and it has indeed been
introduced into our work among single parents. Through our
shop, "Street Level", and our toddler group we made contact
with many single-parent families in need. We noticed that both
the Old Testament and the New said that the people of God
should have a concern for widows and orphans (see Exodus
22:22, Deuteronomy 26:12, Psalm 68:5, James 1:27), and so we
began to wonder how we should respond to this. We concluded
that single parents and their children were a modern-day
equivalent of widows and orphans (of course, there are still actual
widows and orphans to be cared for too). We felt that we should
make these people a priority group. The success of the A-Teams
project suggested that a similar approach would be helpful here.
The idea was that small groups of women and children should
meet together for help, support and friendship.

We started the PACT (Parents and Children Together) groups
in much the same way as we had started the A-Teams, by
contacting one person and getting them to interest their friends in
the idea of a group. As with the A-Teams, we provided a pair of
workers for each group. With the help of the local Area Health
Authority we were able to provide play equipment and facilities
at "Street Level". The early signs are that the PACT groups will
be just as successful as the A-Teams. It also looks as if many other
adult peer groups and interest groups can be formed. The
evangelistic opportunities within these groups are enormous.

5.5   A biblical strategy

While I was studying the New Testament to find examples of mission strategy, two well-known stories from the gospels spoke to me in a powerful new way.

In Matthew 10, Mark 6 and Luke 9 we read that Jesus commissioned the twelve disciples to go out into Israel to proclaim the Kingdom. In Luke 10 we read that He gave the same commission to seventy-two disciples. In both outreaches He gave them a clear strategy to follow. All the teaching I had previously heard about these passages had concentrated almost entirely on the calling and authority that Jesus gave the disciples; I had never heard anyone speak about the basic strategy with which He provided them. As I reread the passages I was surprised to find so much about strategy in them.

Having authorized and empowered His disciples to speak and act on His behalf, Jesus sent them out in twos. As they went they were to bear in mind the urgency and importance of their mission; they were not to waste valuable time in greeting friends and relations along the way.

During their outreach they were to depend on God and, interestingly enough, they were also to depend for food and shelter on the people among whom they would work. Arriving at a town, the disciples, still in pairs, were to search for someone who would listen to them. Having found this "worthy person" or "man of peace", they were to stay with him, receiving from him whatever food and shelter he had to offer (Matthew 10:11; Luke 10:6). They were not to go from house to house but were to preach the Kingdom, heal the sick, raise the dead, cast out demons and cleanse lepers. They were not to seek lots of support and thus dissipate their time and energy; they were instead to do quality work in one household at a time.

This strategy was taken on by the Early Church after Pentecost as their main approach to evangelism. Paul, the outstanding church planter of the New Testament, used basically the same strategy as the twelve and the seventy-two had used, in his missionary efforts around the Roman Empire. He always worked with a partner – first Barnabas and then Silas. He went out without any means of support other than his tent-making skills. He searched for responsive people, first in the synagogues and then beyond. He had to learn this strategy from someone. I believe he was taught by other believers who had already been using it effectively for some time.

I was fascinated to find so many biblical precedents for the strategy we had been using in our small groups projects. When one of our workers starts an A-Team he finds someone who is responsive to him personally and with whom he can form a relationship. The worker then becomes dependent upon this person to provide him with further contacts – that is, his or her group of friends, who form the A-Team. Once the A-Team is formed, the worker stays with it, building lasting relationships in which he can proclaim and demonstrate the Kingdom of God.

If we are to fulfil the commission which Jesus has given us – that is, to reach the world, including apparently hostile places like the inner cities, with His Gospel – we need methods of evangelism that work well. Many of the Church's most tried and trusted methods rely on a provider-client relationship and some sort of in-drag. As a result the effectiveness of the Church's evangelism is severely limited. The strategy and methods of Jesus and the apostles are based on different principles and produce better and longer-lasting results.

6

Taking the Gospel on to the Streets

6.1 Taking the first step

At All Saints our A-Teams project had been running successfully for some time, but we became aware that there was more to outreach than that. It was one thing to be familiar with the basic strategy God had given us, but it was another thing to be aware of the urgent call to reach those who were without hope, and to be fired with the desire to proclaim the Gospel. God did not want us to rest content where we were, but wanted to take us further, challenging our essentially comfortable and uncomplicated lives. On one occasion, when I was preparing the sermon for an evening service, I sensed God telling me to send the congregation out to speak to people, as He guided us.

So at the evening service, I asked the congregation to do just that – to go out in pairs and call on the people whom God told them to visit. Of course, I had to do it too! We went our separate ways in some trepidation.

I felt that I should go and see a couple named Paul and Hilary, who lived in my street. I went to their house with my heart in my mouth, hoping they would be out. I knocked, Paul opened the door and I blurted out something about God having sent me to talk to him about His love. Surprisingly, he invited me in! Paul said he was glad I had called because there were some things he wanted to discuss with me. We had a cup of tea and chatted about the change which had taken place in the lives of their teenage children, who had recently become Christians. At the end of the evening, Paul and Hilary seemed interested in meeting again and so we set up a Basics Course at All Saints where people like them could bring their questions and explore the key elements of the Christian faith.

Paul takes up the story, six months later:

Hilary and I committed ourselves to the Lord about six months ago. Prior to that I was a non-practising member of another faith. I had a vague belief, but absolutely no understanding of God. Hilary's case was less complicated: she was an atheist – full stop. However, our three children Cathal, Liam and Grianne, had recently become Christians and regularly attended All Saints Church. Cathal, our eldest, was particularly committed.

My own conversion came about only when I was broken – this is the case with many people. Jesus pours out His blessings on the halt and the lame – and believe me, I was very halt and very lame. I had no direction, no hope and no happiness. My emotional life was in turmoil due to the break-up of my previous unhappy marriage. I was burdened with fear, guilt and insecurity. I really felt I had the King Midas syndrome in reverse – everything I touched (including gold) turned to dust! My solution to all this pain and unhappiness was alcohol – which, of course, only added to the problem. Finally, in a daze of desperation, I found myself discussing my bankrupt life with Mike.

Hilary and I went on one of All Saints' "Basics" courses, and this reintroduced me to God. Not a God of vengeance and retribution but a God of unlimited love – love for me! What proof is there of His love? He let His Son be murdered for me! Would you or I be willing to pay a price like that? I think we all know the answer to that one.

I was joyfully surprised to find Hilary walking with me on this new road in life. From then on blessings descended on us in a deluge. All our seemingly insoluble problems have been, or are being, solved. Our family grows more united in love by the day. My alcohol problem has been lifted. Life now has a meaning and a purpose. Happiness is ours for the first time in our lives. How has all this come about? The answer is so simple that I failed to see it for over forty years. The life which God and His Son Jesus give is a happy, fulfilled life. Nothing else works. It's as simple as that.

6.2 Taking things further – on to the streets

This experience of reaching out challenged and disturbed me because it showed that our evangelism, no matter how well thought out and planned, was worthless if it didn't flow from a genuine desire to reach people where they were. Just after Easter 1989 I borrowed a church member's campa van and went off to the mountains of South Wales to spend a week alone, praying and thinking through the full implications of this. During that week it became clear that God was calling me to preach on the streets of our local community. God wanted me to lead the way by demonstrating to the church the need for boldness and dependence upon Him, even if this meant doing things in a way which we would find uncomfortable. As I prayed, I could see myself walking around the parish with a large wooden cross, preaching to the passers by. I assumed this was an allegorical picture, but when I asked God what it meant, the only answer I seemed to get was that this was what I should actually do. I was

---

- *Stop* – I had to stop what I was doing before I could know what God wanted us to do about evangelism.

- *Look* – I had to be honest and recognize that strategy is not effective without God's motivating love.

- *Listen* – I had to draw aside and listen to what God was saying.

panic-stricken! I spent the rest of the week trying to convince myself and God that either He or I was mistaken!

Eventually, I had to come to terms with the fact that this was God's clear call to me to preach on the streets of our local community. Carrying a cross would be uncomfortable for me in more ways than one, but it would demonstrate both our dependency on God and the need for boldness in the church's witness.

I was determined to do what God had told me to do, but I also felt fearful and inadequate. The plan was to walk around the parish with a large wooden cross, accompanied by anyone else from the church who was prepared to come with me. I knocked together a large, rough wooden cross for the purpose.

On the day I had set aside to start this ministry, I was so anxious that I could hardly lift the cross, even though it didn't weigh that much. I walked around with it in the church car park, where no one could see me, for about ten minutes, before I had the courage actually to walk out on to the street. I walked to the shops, with two people who were just as scared as I was, and there I began to preach. Not much happened that day, but as the days turned into weeks and the weeks turned into months and the number of people accompanying me grew, some exciting things began to happen. On some days we just prayed as we walked with the cross, asking those we met if they had any prayer requests. Quite a number of people were prayed for on the street, and some of those prayers were answered immediately. Some people were healed of sicknesses and others received a sense of God's presence and peace. We became a familiar sight in Brixton.

In the light summer evenings we visited the courtyards of the council housing blocks, clearing up litter and preaching as we went. As we walked past one of these blocks, two identical heads popped out of a window on the top floor. The twin sisters, Sati and Veena, asked us what we were doing. When we told them they invited us in to talk. After a number of subsequent visits they became Christians and were later baptized in the church.

Preparing a street sermon

When you are preparing your sermon you should bear in mind the fact that three to five minutes seems to be the maximum attention span of the average listener on the street. When preaching in this context it is important to use short sentences, simple ideas and memorable Bible verses.

Here are my notes for a typical street sermon. It is based on John 14:6.

Hello. My name is Mike Breen and I am the Vicar of All Saints Church.

1. Do you know where you are going in your life? Do you have a direction and a purpose? Are you stuck in a rut or are you on the road to life? If you want direction and purpose Jesus is the way. He said, "I am the way and the truth and the life."

2. Do you have certainty in your life or is everything constantly changing? Do you know what is right and what is wrong or are you confused? Jesus said, "I am the truth." That means that He can give us certainty and show us what is right and wrong.

3. Do you feel that life is worth living? Do you fear death? Are you uncertain about what happens after the grave? Jesus said, "I am the life."

4. Do you wish that you knew God? Do you wish that you knew His presence in your life every day? Jesus said, "No one comes to the Father except through me." If you want to know God personally for yourself, then only Jesus can open the way.

5. There are people here on the street who would be glad to talk with you some more about this. If you would like prayer for healing or for anything else, we would be happy to do that here, or we could arrange a time to meet you.

The work with the cross created a groundswell of evangelism in the parish. Within a few months we had two teams, each with a cross, visiting different parts of the parish on Sunday afternoons. We called them Strike Teams. Even those who felt unable to take part in this work were encouraged by it to be bolder in their witnessing, and as a result the number of people coming to the services increased.

The effect on the local community has been very marked. I believe that God has turned over the soil in the locality. He has sown seed and ploughed it in, and as I write I can see a harvest coming up. I see this as the fulfilment of a Bible promise given to me on the last day of my week in South Wales: "Sow for yourselves righteousness, reap the fruit of unfailing love and break up your unploughed ground, for it is time to seek the Lord until he comes and showers righteousness on you" (Hosea 10:12).

God had called us to break up the hard ground of our lives which had prevented them from working in the way that He wanted. Now we could say, "This is the Lord's doing, and it is marvellous in our eyes" (Matthew 21:42).

6.3 Home-grown tracts

Before starting the outreach on the streets I wrote a small tract to give away to the people I would meet. I find that "imported" tracts are rarely as relevant or effective as "home-grown" ones. My tract is reproduced below.

The way to faith

Admit your need for God.
Everybody has a God-shaped hole in the heart
that only He can fill.
(Isaiah 55:6)
Admit your need for forgiveness.
All of us miss the target of God's perfection.
(Romans 3:23)

Believe that Jesus is the answer to your
need for God.
Only Jesus can fill your God-shaped hole.
(John 14:6)
Believe that Jesus is the answer to your
need for forgiveness.
Jesus took away all our sins on the cross,
like a dustbin man taking away our rubbish.
(2 Corinthians 5:21)

Count the cost of being a Christian.
It's difficult to follow Jesus.
(Luke 9:23–24)
Commit yourself to following Jesus.
Once you've started, it's no good giving up.
(Philippians 3:13–14)

> Make a Decision to follow Jesus.
> Following Jesus can mean going in the opposite
> direction to everybody else.
> (Matthew 4:19–20)
> Become a Disciple of Jesus.
> Being a disciple means learning to be like Jesus.
> (John 14:15)
>
> Exchange your life for His.
> Our life is empty and ends in death.
> His life is full and goes on forever.
> (1 John 5:11–12)
> Experience the power of His Spirit.
> His Spirit is the power for life that we need.
> (Ephesians 1:13)

6.4   A pattern for outreach

We started our street outreach piecemeal, without much apparent order or structure, but now, after we have been engaged in outreach for some time, we are able to discern a pattern to it all. Firstly, each individual member of the church can become involved in evangelism and share in the responsibility of reaching and discipling others. Clearly, those members with specific evangelistic gifts are more likely to be at the "frontline" of mission, but everyone, whether they realize it or not, is a witness to the faith they hold.

Secondly, our objective at All Saints is to spread our net as widely as possible, and to make it as easy as we can for a person to come into contact with Christians who can form relationships with them and share with them the message and power of the Gospel.

Once people are contacted, either through organized outreach in the parish or through personal contact with members of the church, they can become involved in the life of the church in many different ways. If they are young, they can join an A-Team; if they are single parents, they can join a PACT group; if they are into music they could go along to the "jammin" session on Monday nights, and so on. If someone becomes interested in learning about God and the Good News of Christ, they can join a Basics Course (an outline of which is included as an appendix to this book). Once a person is contacted there should be more than one way for them to hear the Gospel and to decide to follow Christ.

Finally, we have learned that methods of evangelism are very important, but it has to be said that they have little effect if they are used by people who have not learned to allow the Holy Spirit to empower them and to give them boldness for mission. Even the apostles, who had been trained by the Lord Jesus Himself, still needed to receive God's power before they could carry out the task of evangelizing the world. In fact, Jesus instructed His disciples to wait for this empowering before they began this mission (Acts 1:8). I believe that God wants His people to deepen their desire for His empowering, to be more dependent on Him and to grow in their expectations of what He will do. Schemes alone will never do.

7

Structures for Growth

7.1 Structure is important

Psalm 127:1 says, "Unless the Lord builds the house, its builders labour in vain." We should always remember that God is the builder of our churches, not us. I believe that God is not only interested in the structures for growth outlined in this chapter but is actually positively promoting them. My experience leads me to the conclusion that if applied sensitively, thoroughly and with humility towards God, the structures which have been revealed to us can allow God to do His work of building the Church.

There are practical reasons why churches, whether they be in the inner city or in the suburbs, do not see growth. Either their programmes do not contact enough people or their structures are not capable of sustaining a large membership. In this chapter I will explain the structures which have enabled All Saints to grow.

People can more easily feel at home in a small group than in a larger one. So when a church grows it is essential to have small groups, since without them people will feel less involved, less supported and more vulnerable. As a consequence of this, inertia will grow and growth will slow down. This is particularly true in an urban area, where people's daily experience often involves high levels of pressure and stress. Often people find themselves lonely and unsupported – even isolated – within a highly complex and sometimes hostile environment. Being a member of a church should in some ways counteract these negative effects for the individual.

Many of the churches in urban areas are what I call "family-like churches". They have a membership of about forty or fifty and are organized and led according to the unwritten rules of the family. These churches are able to grow only as far as the family relationships within them will allow. They are highly resistant to growth because of the pressures which growth produces within their internal structure. However, these family-like churches are particularly good at taking on specific tasks within the local community – for example, running a Sunday School or providing pastoral care for an old people's home. They are usually very friendly to outsiders and present themselves to the world as being ready to receive new members, but in practice they only receive enough new members to replace those who leave. This means that these churches remain static in size over long periods of time. In many inner-city areas cultural, class and racial divisions further complicate the situation. It is not surprising that there are few inner-city churches which really overcome these barriers.

In recent years a three-level church structure made up of cell groups, congregations and celebrations has become widespread, particularly in the house church movement. This can be an effective way of structuring churches for growth. However, my research into this subject has shown me that there is in fact great resistance to this approach in many inner-city churches. Small groups may be the best way of meeting people's needs, but their effects are also potentially damaging to the family-like church. Small groups are sometimes seen as a threat to the total fellowship of such churches. Splitting a church into groups means that not everyone is in contact with everyone else. The normal means of communication and support which exist in the church are threatened. This can mean that any small groups which do get off the ground become peripheral, optional extras which are not linked in to the main programme of the church.

7.2 The Household Church

When I joined All Saints it was one of these family-like churches. I was aware of both the people's desire for the church to grow and the inbuilt resistance to growth. I decided to use the desire for growth as a starting-point, and to explain the sacrifices that would need to be made in order for this growth to take place. The church leaders and I spent some time seeking guidance from God, and gradually a vision of the way we should go emerged. As it became clearer the leaders and I became personally committed to seeing it fulfilled, and we also became more closely committed to one another. There was a corporate decision amongst the leadership to make whatever sacrifices were necessary. The Bible says that without a vision the people cast off restraint (Proverbs 29:18). The positive implication of this is that when they have a vision the people take on proper restraint. This is what happened at All Saints.

- *Stop* working and hoping for church growth without any thought of church structure.

- *Look* at the current structures and identify the inbuilt barriers to growth.

- *Listen* to what God is saying about restructuring.

The leaders and I put this shared vision down on paper and presented it to the church as the basis for a five-year plan for growth. In this document we described the structures and programmes which we felt were necessary in order for growth to come to the church. Its introduction said:

The basic vision is, as we often pray, that God's Kingdom will come to Brixton Hill. This will mean that All Saints must grow – our understanding of God and of His Kingdom must grow, and our relevance and significance in the community must grow. If this happens, more people will start to come to All Saints as

God calls them into His Kingdom. This is what God wants and what the community needs – there is no reason why the church shouldn't have between five hundred and a thousand members within five years.

At each Annual General Meeting of the church since then the vision has been re-presented and a plan for the new church year has been proposed.

Household Groups
Because of this jointly held vision of a growing, healthy, dynamic

---

How to structure a Household Group evening

- *8.00 p.m.: Welcome.* Make everyone, especially new people, feel comfortable and welcome. Offer them tea or coffee.

- *8.30 p.m.: Worship.* Draw the people into intimate communion with God. The worship leader must be a true worshipper him/herself.

- *Prayer, listening to God and sharing.* Encourage people to share what they have received from God. You may need to take the first step. Share the exciting and challenging things which God is doing.

- *20–30 minutes of teaching/input.* Draw people to Jesus. The people should be able to go away with a thought or idea which they can put into practice in their lives.

- *Prayer and healing.* Share needs and words of knowledge.

- *10.00 p.m.: Informal.* Drinks and food, fellowship. People should be preparing to leave.

church, we were able to build a structure for growth. In the course of the first year much of our time, effort and resources went into establishing small groups. We called them "Household Groups", since we wanted to emphasize that they were supposed to be life-sharing and family-like. We also wanted parents and children to meet together in these groups where possible. To underline the importance of the groups we called All Saints "the Household Church".

In the early stages of the development of the Household Groups at All Saints, the teaching material was provided centrally and distributed weekly in the form of notes. Since then the responsibility for teaching has been in the hands of the group leaders. Below is an example of the sort of planning sheet which the group leaders used to be given. In the original there were spaces for the leaders to write in their own thoughts and ideas.

7.3   A three-level church

So now the basic units in the structure of All Saints are small groups. We call these groups the primary level of church life. The secondary level is the congregations, each of which is made up of four or more Household Groups. The tertiary level of church life is the celebrations at which all the congregations meet together. Of course, there is a need for a tertiary level only when there is more than one congregation. When a congregation, through growth, includes sufficient people to form four more Household Groups, then a new congregation can be started.

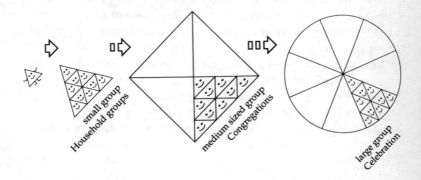

As All Saints has grown and developed a number of congregations have come into being. On a typical Sunday the programme would look like this:

9.00 a.m. Early morning Communion, attended by those who prefer a quiet service, and by shift workers who cannot make it to church at any other time. Communions for the sick and the elderly are sent out from this service. This is not a congregation in the sense meant above, but is simply a means of providing Communion for the whole church at the beginning of the day.

10.00 a.m. This congregation was established in the autumn of 1989 and focuses its ministry and outreach on those who prefer a more traditional service.

11.30 a.m. This is the mother of all the other congregations. It is based around a ministry to families and children.

7.00 p.m. This is the newest congregation and is intended for teenagers and young adults.

No one is expected to go to church more than once on a Sunday, but each person is encouraged to attend his or her own congregation regularly.

On the first Sunday of each month at 11.30 a.m. all the congregations come together for a joint celebration. The service is centred on Holy Communion and includes elements from each of the different services.

We also used to hold a teaching service on Wednesday evenings as a supplement to the Sunday programme. In September 1990 we dispensed with these teaching services, in order to release the church from dependence upon my teaching and to encourage the whole body to engage in this ministry. This change has led to an enriching of the Household Groups and the Sunday congregations.

So when we began in 1987, All Saints was a small, friendly, single-level church supporting a number of activities such as Bible study groups. Today it is a three-level church structured around Household Groups, congregations and celebrations. Maintaining this structure is not difficult, because it not only guides the growth of the church but in many ways promotes it.

7.4   A three-dimensional church

All Saints is not only a three-level church but also a three-dimensional church. If a church is to have a healthy life it needs to be three-dimensional – that is, it needs to have an upward dimension, which is expressed most clearly in worship and prayer, an inward dimension, seen in fellowship and pastoral care, and an outward dimension, seen in evangelism and social action.

A healthy church must have a three-dimensional life

1. An upward dimension towards God

2. An inward dimension towards the Church

3. An outward dimension towards the world

A healthy church also needs a structure.

Each of these dimensions needs to be expressed as fully as possible at each level of the church's life. Because Household Groups are the basic units of the church they must include each of the dimensions of its life. The upward dimension is expressed as a group worships, prays, listens to God and obeys what He is saying. As the group meets with God in this way He will commission them to work in both the inward and outward dimensions.

The inward dimension develops as the group begins to share an open lifestyle. Members feel secure enough to admit their weaknesses and needs without fear of rejection. Household Groups should be life-sharing. As they meet week by week and worship together, God reveals His intention to meet specific needs both naturally and supernaturally – naturally, through the caring concern of the members for one another, and supernaturally, through counsel, healing and prayer. Learning from the Bible and applying its teaching is an important part of the life of the group, but Bible study is not the group's sole function.

The outward dimension is expressed as the group reaches out into the community. Outreach can be done in many different ways, but friend-to-friend contact and small groups are the best methods we have so far discovered.

At the congregational level the three dimensions are expressed in ways similar to those found at the group level. The upward dimension happens as the members of the congregation worship together – singing, praying, listening to God and obeying what He says. Often the worship acts as a springboard into the other two dimensions.

The inward dimension is also seen week by week within the congregation's worship as the people form small groups in order to listen to one another and to pray together, and also informally after the service as people stay behind to chat over a tea or a coffee.

The outward dimension is expressed as the congregation reaches out to the visitors who come to church on Sunday and in corporate outreach events such as outdoor services.

At the celebration level the worship is the upward dimension, while the encouragement and inspiration which the meeting provides is the inward dimension. In addition, the people have opportunities to meet with folk they don't have regular contact with. As for the outward dimension, the event itself is a witness to the community and may include an evangelistic message.

Also there are the ongoing church-wide evangelistic programmes.

The upward dimension is most clearly
expressed in worship and prayer.

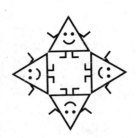

The inward dimension includes pastoral
care and fellowship.

The outward dimension is seen in evangelism and social action.

7.5   Structure, spiritual gifts and ministry

The structure which we have developed at All Saints is helpful not only for facilitating growth but also for releasing ministry gifts. The small groups are a safe environment in which people can exercise spiritual gifts and develop the ministry they have been called to. As a person grows in confidence and effectiveness, so they can be released to minister within the congregation of which the small group is a part. If they have potential for still further development they can be released into ministry across the whole church.

We place a high value upon people seeing the empowering of the Spirit, and we encourage every member of the church to be available to the Spirit's anointing. Our understanding of the spiritual gifts is that Christians are able to receive any and all of the gifts which the Holy Spirit wants to release. This means that we should be available to the Spirit and that we should expect Him to empower us to function in different ways within the body of Christ as He chooses. However, our experience is that the Holy Spirit gives certain gifts to certain people. This should not make us doubt that the Spirit can still release any gift at any time, but rather it should lead us to a growing awareness of the particular ways in which the Spirit is calling us to serve others. If we are not faithfully exercizing the gifts we have been given, how can we expect God to give us more? Once a person becomes aware of their spiritual gifts, they can begin to discern the area of ministry into which they are being called.

The lists of gifts in the New Testament are quite comprehensive (e.g. 1 Corinthians 12:4–11; Romans 12:6–8), but we do not believe they are exhaustive. Rather, we feel they can be used as a guide to the experience of individuals and churches. All ministries, of course, should be seen in relation to the whole body of Christ. Paul makes it clear that ministries are given to a church "to prepare God's people for works of service, so that the body of Christ may be built up until we all reach unity in the faith and in the knowledge of the Son of God and become mature, attaining to the whole measure of the fulness of Christ" (Ephesians 4:12–13). It is important, therefore, that the development of these ministries within the life of a church is encouraged.

From my own experience and from my study of particular individuals in the Bible who functioned in various areas of ministry, I have come to the view that the development of an individual's ministry is shaped by two factors: (1) the spiritual gifts they most regularly receive, and (2) the natural talents which God has developed in them through their background and experience. Bearing these two factors in mind, we can prayerfully move towards a clear definition of a person's ministry. Together all our God-given natural talents and spiritual gifts combine to form a ministry.

Obviously, spiritual gifts must take precedence over talents in the defining of a ministry, because if God began to gift us differently we would start to use a different set of talents and so function in a new ministry role. For example, someone might have a ministry as an evangelist, but if God began to release to that person gifts appropriate to teaching, he or she might stop functioning as an evangelist and instead operate solely as a teacher.

At All Saints we have found the use of "ministry umbrellas" very helpful. A person may not see himself as, for example, a prophet, but perhaps he would be happy to exercise a gift of prophecy if he were standing with others under a prophetic umbrella ministry. This approach releases people from the attitude that they, individually, could never have such a ministry. It also tempers the tendency to see these ministries as "offices" which only certain outstanding individuals can perform.

As people at All Saints have recognized which umbrella they need to stand under, their ministries, operating within a safe environment, have developed and grown. Some have been released into ministries across the whole church. In some cases people have assumed responsibilities which they had never dreamed of. Some of the people under a particular umbrella have a more complete expression of the ministry than others, but everyone under it has a role to play.

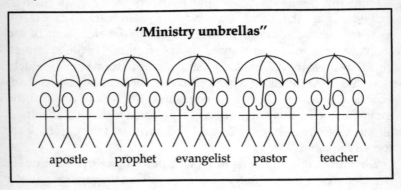

"Ministry umbrellas"

apostle   prophet   evangelist   pastor   teacher

7.6 Conclusion

As a result of the church structure which we have adopted All Saints has grown remarkably. In 1987 there were about 40 regular attenders on Sundays, of whom about a dozen were key, committed members. By September 1990 the Sunday attendance was over 200, about 150 of whom were members of small primary-level groups of one kind or another. In the next few years we expect these figures to increase significantly and rapidly.

8

Leadership

8.1 The skeleton of the Body

I believe that leadership is crucial to the health and vitality of a church. Training others for leadership is one of the most important functions of any leader. John Wimber has described leaders as the skeleton or the key infrastructure of the Body of Christ. The quality and health of the Body depends to a large extent upon the quality and strength of the skeleton. Therefore leaders and potential leaders within a church need to have good training.

Investing in leadership is one of the best things that leaders can do. If a leader is committed to the quantitative and qualitative growth of his church he must also be committed to the training of well-equipped, mature leaders. In my opinion there is a direct relationship between the number of well-trained leaders in a church and its size. The greater the number of leaders, the greater the number of people who can be held in a fellowship at any one time. There is also a relationship between the spiritual maturity of the leaders and that of the church they serve.

8.2 Bert's story

Bert was an orphan. The institutions in which he spent his childhood never satisfied his deep need for love and acceptance. He remembers almost nothing about the first thirteen years of his life except running away many times. At the age of fifteen he decided to strike out on his own and left the "correctional" boarding school where he had been living. He soon got into trouble. His need for love made him vulnerable and easy prey for those who wanted to exploit young men. He found that he could get love and acceptance only from homosexuals, who wanted him for only one thing. In time he escaped from this life. He got married and sought to express himself through the care which he could offer to others as a nurse. Slowly, in various ways, he became aware that God was calling him to Himself. Bert became a committed Christian, and so too did his wife Barbara.

However, many of the problems and hindrances which had been created by his early life had never been resolved, and eventually he became desperate for a solution to them. He felt that his life was in a mess. However, he was still able to hear God. The Lord guided him to leave work, settle his affairs and join a Youth With a Mission (YWAM) discipleship school in New Zealand and Australia. During the seven months which he and Barbara spent there they were profoundly helped. Before their return God told them that they would come back to new situations and opportunities and even to a new locality.

Once they were back in Britain they were invited to join the Shaftesbury Housing Association as wardens. Bert had lived in South London all his life, and when I first met him at a Shaftesbury Wardens' Conference he was living a mile or so away from All Saints. Since joining us about a year after his return to this country Bert has become a key leader within the church. He is very open to others and he is clearly a man in whom God has done a deep work. His humility towards God and other people makes him a prime candidate for leadership: he is easy to work with and to train for additional responsibility.

Bert is one of over twenty leaders who have been called, trained and released into various ministries within the church. Some of them were not even Christians three years ago. The key to this rapid growth in maturity is on-the-job training. For me as a leader there is nothing more important than training others for leadership. Jesus Himself treated it as a very high priority. His ministry is a marvellous example of a leader enabling others to lead.

8.3 Jesus and leadership

Jesus' leadership and method of training leaders were flexible: He adopted different approaches at different times.

Highly directive
In the early stages of His ministry Jesus was extremely directive. "'Come, follow me,' Jesus said [to Simon and Andrew], 'and I will make you fishers of men.' At once they left their nets and followed him" (Mark 1:17-18).

Motivating through vision
When the disciples' initial enthusiasm waned and when they made major mistakes, Jesus was able to offer them security by pointing them in the right direction. He said to them, "Do not be afraid, little flock, for your Father has been pleased to give you the Kingdom" (Luke 12:32). He was always there to lead them out of their difficulties by given them a vision of where they were going.

Increasingly participative
Once their awareness and understanding had grown sufficiently Jesus was able to use much more intimate and participative language to describe His relationship to them. He said, "I am the vine; you are the branches" (John 15:5), and also, "I no longer call you servants . . . Instead, I have called you friends" (v.15).

Delegating responsibility and authority
Finally, Jesus was able to delegate responsibility for His mission to His disciples. He also delegated His authority, ensuring that they understood that He was not withdrawing from involvement but would be available to them in the Person of the Holy Spirit. He said, "Go and make disciples of all nations, baptizing them in the name of the Father and of the Son and of the Holy Spirit, and teaching them to obey everything I have commanded you. And surely I will be with you always, to the very end of the age" (Matthew 28:19–20). He also said, "The Counsellor, the Holy Spirit, whom the Father will send in my name, will teach you all

things and will remind you of everything I have said to you"
(John 14:26).

8.4　Four levels of development

The pattern of leadership which we can see in Jesus' ministry –
that is, the process which begins with calling by the leader and
ends with delegation – is one which can be transferred to
leadership in our churches today. We must encourage the
process by which the people we lead mature in the Christian life
and so take on responsibility for leading others. In order to do this
we must, like Jesus, adopt different styles of leadership at
different times. Using an approach drawn from modern management training, from the four styles of Jesus' leadership I
have devised a simple pattern composed of four levels of
development. It should be borne in mind that these levels may
refer to specific skills or tasks rather than to someone's overall
ability: the fact that they are not ready to lead a housegroup does
not necessarily mean that they cannot be given responsibility for
organizing a rota, for example.

Level 1: TELL

Follower: low in competence and high in confidence.
Leader: strong, clear and directive leadership.

The leader needs to be sensitive to the confidence and competence of the follower at this stage and he should give clear direction as to what needs to be done. The follower's response tends to be childlike.

Example: I asked Bert to help out in a Household Group in a pastoral and teaching capacity.

Level 2: SELL

Follower: low in competence and low in confidence.
Leader: inspirational, visionary and charismatic leadership.

This is a key stage in the follower's development. He has become aware of his basic inability and if he is not handled sensitively he will become discouraged and even more ineffective. The leader now needs to give the follower a clear vision of where the church and he personally are going. The benefits of going through the current pain in order to realize the future vision need to be explained. All this may take a lot of time.

Example: I asked Bert to lead a Household Group of his own. I also put him on the leadership training course, which provided him with a vision of the overall strategy of the church. I began to see him once a week.

Level 3: GEL

Follower: growing in competence and increasing in confidence.
Leader: participative, intimate, relationship-based leadership.

Now the leader needs to spend a lot of time with the follower. His competence and confidence will only increase if the security offered by close interpersonal relationships is available.

Example: Bert now had a public role as a churchwarden. I asked him to team up with the other churchwardens to form a pastoral visiting team.

Level 4: DELegate

Follower: high in competence and high in confidence.
Leader: delegating, administrating, managing leadership.

A person who has reached this level of development can be given overall responsibility for a task. It should be noted that the leader will still need to help the follower review and plan. As far as possible the responsibility for decisions should be put into the hands of the follower.

Example: As the leader of a congregational team, Bert was now released to be trained as the pastor for another church.

Each of the four Levels is roughly parallel to a management style: Level 1 is like *classical leadership*, Level 2 is like *charismatic leadership*, Level 3 is like *human relations leadership* and Level 4 is like *systemic leadership*. Below is a graphic representation of the four Levels, drawn on the axes of intimacy and time spent together.

↑ *Intimacy*

Level 4 (Systemic leadership) Follower: high competence 　　　　　 high confidence Leader: delegate, launch	Level 3 (Human relation leadership) Follower: high competence 　　　　　 increasing confidence Leader: gel, participate
Level 1 (Classical leadership) Follower: low competence 　　　　　 high confidence Leader: tell, direct	Level 2 (Charismatic leadership) Follower: low competence 　　　　　 low confidence Leader: sell, inspire

Time spent together

It should by now be clear that if there is to be maturity and growth within the Body of Christ, different styles of leadership need to be used in different contexts. But most of us are stronger in one style of leadership than we are in others. We may have a definite dislike of some styles, but they may be necessary if the church is to progress from immaturity to maturity. This means that leaders need to learn new styles and unfamiliar methods so that others are equipped to grow. The best leaders are the ones who recognize where people are in their growth and maturity and then act appropriately.

Of course, leadership is not just a matter of one-to-one discipleship but also involves the leading of the whole church and of the various groups within it. The leader will need to recognize the maturity of the group or church and adopt the appropriate style of leadership. This needs to be done sensitively. Problems can arise if some of the people feel that the style of leadership being used is inappropriate to them as individuals. A group as a whole may be quite immature, but some of the individuals within it may be highly trained and experienced. Of course, there is more to spiritual maturity than simply having certain skills and talents, but there may be difficulties if some of the people feel patronized.

In my experience, conflict within churches and groups often arises either when an inappropriate style of leadership is actually used or when strong characters within the church begin to say that the style is inappropriate. Such situations need to be handled carefully. Where numerical growth is occurring, there may be a temptation to respond only to the group and not to some of the individuals. Where numbers are declining or static, there may be a tendency to respond solely to individuals and never to the group as a whole.

8.5 The Body growing towards maturity

In Ephesians 4:11, 16 Paul says that the whole Body needs to be equipped to serve, and that this state of readiness is to be achieved through the exercise of five leadership ministries – those of the apostle, the prophet, the evangelist, the pastor and the teacher. If a leader is committed to equipping his church to grow, he will be concerned to reveal and release these ministries. As they are exercised, maturity and unity – the twin aims of church growth – are promoted.

Jesus said that we were to emulate the simple trust and humility of children (Matthew 18:3), but in Ephesians 4 Paul makes it clear that there are certain aspects of childhood which we should leave behind us (compare 1 Corinthians 13:11). This is what we do as we mature in the faith. The development of maturity, at both the individual level and the corporate one, is a process, not an event. Leaders need to recognize this process and seek to engage in it and with it so that the church can grow continuously.

In the parable of the growing seed (Mark 4:26-29) Jesus speaks about the growth of the Kingdom and encourages us to be patient. It is a fact that however much we understand the process of growth, we still need to be patient both with ourselves and with others as growth takes place.

In His parable Jesus indicates that there are three stages of growth: "the stalk", "the ear" and "the full kernel in the ear". I believe that these stages are similar to childhood, adolescence and adulthood.

In his first Epistle the Apostle John also recognizes three stages of growth in the people he is writing to: he addresses children, young men and fathers. I believe that he is giving different advice, encouragement and teaching to people at different stages of spiritual growth:

I write to you, dear children, because your sins have been forgiven on account of His name.

I write to you, fathers, because you have known Him who is from the beginning.

I write to you, young men, because you have overcome the evil one.

I write to you, dear children, because you have known the Father.

I write to you, fathers, because you have known Him who is from the beginning.

I write to you, young men, because you are strong, and the word of God lives in you, and you have overcome the evil one.

The process of growth from childhood to adulthood is what needs to take place if a person is to develop into a leader, and also if a church is to develop a corporate maturity.

8.6 Seven areas of growth

Ephesians 4:13 shows us that maturing churches and individuals need to see growth in a number of areas – they are unity, faith, knowledge, identity, purpose, security and responsibility. We need to consider each of these in turn within the context of development from childhood to adulthood.

Unity

A modern-day definition of unity is interdependence. This is one of the main goals of growth within the Body of Christ. To arrive at this adult state, we first have to recognize that we begin in the childlike state of dependence. All children are dependent upon their parents: they rely on them to provide everything they need. From this position of dependence children grow into adolescents, who are usually seeking independence from authority figures. Similarly, after the first stage of their Christian life believers move from a dependence upon their leaders and authority figures to seeking their own way. However, this independence is not the final goal. The adolescent Christian needs to develop into a mature adult living in interdependence with others – he must be someone who not only recognizes that others need him but also knows that he needs others. This process of growth can be summarized thus:

Childhood	dependence (apparent inequality)
Adolescence	independence (seeking equality)
Adulthood	interdependence (united with others as an equal)

A leader should seek to give the security and challenge necessary to enable a person to move from dependence through independence to interdependence.

Faith

In order for faith to be fully active and alive within a person, often the alternatives to faith need to be experienced. A child in the faith often finds rules and laws helpful as he begins to integrate his new-found experience of God into his lifestyle. However, this can soon develop into legalism, and this, as Paul points out in Romans, causes desperation and an experience of "death". Rules in themselves can be useful as a means of establishing priorities, but as soon as they develop into a legalistic structure they become worse than useless. Often, when this legalism is thrown off, it is replaced by licence. Christians who do this are like adolescents who want to break out of rules and regulations, and rebel against traditions and structures. However, such rebellion is not the goal: rather, that goal is a faith in Christ which is lived out in a person's lifestyle.

Childhood	legalism (rules rapidly develop into law)
Adolescence	licence (breaking out, rebelling)
Adulthood	lifestyle (living by faith and establishing your everyday priorities through your relationship with Christ)

A leader will need to model a consistent lifestyle which others can emulate and learn from.

Knowledge

This biblical term means wisdom gained through experience. In the childhood stage of development a believer is often ignorant about many areas of the Christian life. The adolescent stage is marked by a quest for information. Really this is "head knowledge" which has not as yet become "heart knowledge" because it has not been tried and tested. A mature Christian is one who has a knowledge and wisdom which he can apply to the various situations of life.

Childhood	ignorance
Adolescence	information ("head knowledge" which has not yet been tried and tested by experience)
Adulthood	knowledge (wisdom based on information and experience – *epignosis* in Greek)

Leaders, particularly those with a gift of teaching, will need to ensure that the imparting and receiving of information does not become the ultimate goal of their ministry.

Identity (measuring up to Christ)
The process of growing to maturity includes identifying with Christ or, as Paul puts it, "attaining to the whole measure of the fulness of Christ" (Ephesians 4:13) or growing up "into him who is the Head" (v.15). This growth in identity, flowing from an identification with Christ, begins with an awareness in the infant Christian that his identity is given. Children are born into a household, are given a name and grow up in an environment which provides them with identity. Similarly, infant Christians have an identity which is derived from those around them. In the intermediate stage of growth the Christian begins to seek his own identity, just like the adolescent who says, "I want to be me". One of the key tests of maturity is whether or not the person has found his identity. A mature Christian will have to come to understand that his identity flows from his unique and special relationship with Christ.

Childhood	identity is given (others say who you are)
Adolescence	identity is sought ("I want to be me")
Adulthood	identity is found ("attaining to the whole measure of the fulness of Christ" means identifying with Him and finding all you need in Him)

The followers' goal should be the imitation of Christ and not the imitation of the leader. However, their imitation of Christ will begin with an imitation of the leader's imitation of Him.

Purpose and direction

As a Christian matures in his faith there will be a growing purpose and direction in his life. Without this he is liable to be "tossed back and forth by the waves, and blown here and there by every wind of teaching" (Ephesians 4:14). He will be like a ship which has neither rudder nor anchor: it drifts in the water and is blown around by the storms that come its way. Immature Christians, like children, depend upon being given a purpose and direction by others. This means that they can be influenced for good or for bad. In the intermediate stage the Christian begins to seek his own way. In the mature stage he finds his direction and purpose in his relationship with Christ.

Childhood	purpose and direction are given (influences can be for good or bad)
Adolescence	purpose and direction are sought (find your own way in the world)
Adulthood	purpose and direction are found (you know what to do and how to do it)

In the early stages leaders should not shrink from being directive. Young Christians need direction: they need to know what it is to be a disciple of Jesus. They see this best in the lives of others, and they often need to be told how they can be the same. As the Christian progresses he will need the courage to try discipleship for himself and the humility still to listen to others. Leaders need to be able to give clear direction in the initial stages and to delegate more and more responsibility to the person as time goes on.

Security

An experience of the twin realities of love and truth leads to a growth in the individual's security. An infant Christian who receives little or intermittent love and discipline ends up being insecure, because he doesn't know how to make decisions or who or what to trust. The Christian's adolescence is marked by the person seeking security outside the bounds of what is familiar. An adult Christian is secure because he has an understanding of truth and love (i.e. how to give it and receive it) and is prepared to share them without condition in order to build others up.

Childhood	security is given (love and truth are received and returned according to what is given)
Adolescence	security is sought (love and truth need to be redefined)
Adulthood	security is found (you know what love and truth are, and you are prepared to give both without condition for the building up of others)

The leader needs to ensure that even those Christians who rebel are not able to escape the security of forgiveness and the boundaries of love.

Responsibility (doing our part)

Being responsible means understanding your role and taking steps to fulfil it. An infant Christian has little or no responsibility. An adolescent knows what is expected of him but often tries to "duck out". Adult Christians are prepared to do their part so that the enterprise in which they are involved succeeds and others are supported within it.

Childhood	unresponsible (someone takes responsibilty for you)
Adolescence	irresponsible (you have realized that responsibility is difficult and requires discipline and sacrifice)
Adulthood	responsible (you are prepared to do your part for the betterment and building up of others)

If those we lead are not given responsibility they will never learn to take it. Growing Christians should be free to make mistakes: "If a job is worth doing, it's worth doing badly."

8.7 The qualities of leadership

Up to this point I have concentrated on the methods and means of leadership, but now I want to discuss the qualities which are needed in leaders.

Servants

If we spend quality time and energy on our leaders and are committed to their personal growth they will feel valued and special, which is a positive thing. They are special, but if they are to be effective they must have an attitude of servanthood, which is the most important leadership quality. On many occasions, such as the one when He washed the disciples' feet (John 13), Jesus demonstrated that leaders must be servants. He said, "Whoever wants to become great among you must be your servant, and whoever wants to be first must be slave of all. For even the Son of Man did not come to be served, but to serve, and to give his life as a ransom for many" (Mark 10:43–45). Recognizing that leaders are servants is the key to understanding the qualities of biblical leadership.

Shepherds

Being a shepherd is another vital part of what it is to be a leader. In John 10 Jesus calls Himself "the good shepherd" (vv. 11, 14): since He is the model for all leaders, they too must be shepherds. He says a shepherd:

- knows his sheep
- calls them by name
- leads them out
- goes on ahead of them
- lays down his life for them

In John 21 Jesus tells Peter that he must be a shepherd. He says to him:

- "Feed my lambs."
- "Take care of my sheep."
- "Feed my sheep."
- "Follow me!"

In 1 Peter 5 the Apostle himself affirms that all leaders are shepherds under the chief shepherd, Christ. He says shepherds or overseers should:

- serve the flock
- be willing to serve
- not be greedy, but be eager to serve
- not dominate the flock
- be examples

These passages, particularly 1 Peter 5, seem to be written with Ezekiel 34 in mind. This chapter talks about the wicked shepherds of Israel who:

- take care of themselves
- make what they can out of the sheep
- do not strengthen the weak
- do not heal the sick
- do not bind up the injured
- do not seek the strays and the lost
- do not protect the flock from enemies

Interestingly, Ezekiel reveals that the sheep who are treated in this way by the shepherds *become like them:* they consider themselves more important than others and put their own needs first (Ezekiel 34:17, 20).

Leaders in the Church should function as shepherds, but they should never forget that they are also sheep. Leaders should be:

- followers first
- servants second
- leaders last

Jesus, the chief shepherd, is also the Lamb of God. He does only what He sees His Father doing (John 5:19). In so doing, He leads all of us. The fact is that we are all both followers and leaders. Viewed from the front, all Christians are sheep; viewed from behind, we are all shepherds. So we should be aware of who we are following and who is following us.

Spirit-filled
As well as being servants and shepherds, leaders should also be Spirit-filled. Jesus Himself had His ministry confirmed as the Spirit came upon Him in the form of a dove (Luke 3:21–22). He came back from His temptations in the wilderness full of the Holy Spirit (Luke 4:1, 14). He promised His disciples that they too would be filled so that they could be His witnesses (Luke 24:49; Acts 1:8). If leaders function as Spirit-filled servants and shepherds of the people, the Church has every opportunity to become the mature body of believers which God desires.

8.8 Training on the job
Jesus had only three years to inaugurate the Kingdom and to train and equip His disciples. Although it is clear that He drew aside with them from time to time, He must have done most of the training, teaching and pastoral care which they needed on the job in the cut-and-thrust of establishing the Kingdom. This is a good working model for us. If people need training, help and care, we should take them with us, sharing our ministry as much as possible. I believe that this approach will lead to the raising up of quality leaders who are committed to the growth and maturity of others – leaders who are prepared to lay down their lives for the sheep, who will grow to maturity in the Spirit.

8.9   Urban church leadership

In the urban areas of this country responsibility for the life of the community has been removed from the local people. This has often led to a vacuum in community leadership and has exacerbated the general problem of powerlessness. A lack of vision and direction has contributed to the "everyone for himself" attitude, and has prevented the identifiction and training of leaders. A commitment in the church to the training of leaders will eventually benefit the whole community, as the church makes its mark and the Kingdom is demonstrated through people who are becoming more hopeful and certain about the direction in which they are going.

The vacuum in local Christian leadership has led professional clergymen and other church leaders to respond either with a paternalistic style of leadership or with a non-directive one. The paternalistic approach prevents other leaders from being identified and trained, because everything is dependent on the single leader at the top. The non-directive approach also has a negative effect on leadership, because the group is king and consensus is the only policy. However, strong, flexible leadership will lead to the identification, equipping and releasing of more and more leaders, and so the tragedy of the declining urban church will then be reversed.

Epilogue

On Mount Horeb Moses said to God, "You have been telling me, 'Lead these people', but you have not let me know whom you will send with me." The Lord replied, "My Presence will go with you, and I will give you rest." The desert was the classroom in which Moses and the people of Israel learned how to listen to God and to follow His Presence. Similarly, All Saints has become a church of "desert dwellers" following the Lord's Presence through the spiritual desert of dependence upon Him and through the physical desert of the inner city. God continues to develop and deepen our life together, and from time to time we "break camp" and move on to a whole new area of experience and understanding.

We at All Saints are continuing to move ahead in the areas which have been described in this book, but we are finding that the basic principles we have discovered remain valid. Indeed, they are becoming ever more certain as we continually return to them and test their value in the everyday life of our church. My hope is that what I have shared in this book will provide a stimulus for your prayer and thinking as you consider what God is doing in your church. God is calling us to prepare and make ready for all that this decade will bring. I hope that in some small way this book will help you in your preparation.

I believe that if we listen we can hear the voice of the Lord saying, "In the desert prepare a way for the Lord; make straight in the wilderness a highway for our God. Every valley shall be raised up, every mountain and hill made low; the rough ground shall become level, the rugged places a plain. And the glory of the

Lord will be revealed, and all mankind will see it together"
(Isaiah 40:3–5). God has promised that those who recognize that
the desert is their home will be blessed. The featureless landscape
of the desert, which is so difficult to map or to find a way through,
will have running through it a road called "the Way of Holiness",
where protection, joy and gladness will be found (Isaiah 35:8–10).

We must recognize that we each live in a desert, that hearing
God's word for us now is the only way to find that Way of
Holiness, and that all other roads lead to desperation and death.
Finding God's way by listening to Him through prayer and
individual and corporate Scripture reading is not an option, but a
vital necessity. Deserts are dangerous places.

As we continue in the desert we will find that the thirsty
ground will become living water and the arid sand an oasis
(Isaiah 35:1–2, 7). Even though we live in a desert we can be
strong and fearless because God is with us (verses 3–6).

Our desert experiences are intended to give us a "desert
mentality" which leads us to rely on God fully and firmly. We can
know how to pray, "Give us today our daily bread", remembering that Jesus Himself is the Bread of Life and our Leader
through the wilderness. A desert mentality does not expect
disaster and doom, but rather God's blessing. It is not con-
ditioned and made rigid by previous experiences, but is instead
disciplined into expecting God to provide something fresh for
everyone on every occasion. He has said, "Forget the former
things; do not dwell on the past. See, I am doing a new thing!
Now it springs up; do you not perceive it? I am making a way in
the desert and streams in the wasteland" (Isaiah 43:18–19).

This desert mentality was surely what Jesus was talking about
in the Sermon on the Mount, when He described His disciples as
participating in two apparently contradictory realities (Matthew
5:3–11). Even though we are in a desert – poor in spirit,
mourning, meek, hungry and thirsty for God, merciful, pure in
heart, peacemakers and persecuted – we are blessed. This
blessing is seen as the Kingdom of God comes among us like

streams in the desert. Jesus, our new Moses, will lead us through this experience until we eventually reach the Promised Land – the consummation of His Kingdom at His return.

Appendix

A Basics Course

At All Saints we run Basics Courses for people who want to know about the Christian faith. Below is a reproduction of the leaflet which we use as the basis of the courses.

God the Father

God created the world.	Genesis 1:1; Psalm 19:1–2
God created you and me.	Genesis 1:26–27; Psalm 139:13
God created us for a purpose.	Genesis 1:26–27; Mark 12:30

We all have a God-shaped hole in the heart which only He can fill.
We can know Him as our Father.   Psalm 103:13

Jesus taught us to pray to the Father like this:

Our Father in heaven,
May your holy name be honoured;
may your Kingdom come;
may your will be done on earth
as it is in heaven.
Give us today the food we need.
Forgive us the wrongs we have done,
as we forgive the wrongs
that others have done to us.
Do not bring us to hard testing,
but keep us safe from the evil one.

Jesus

No one seriously doubts that Jesus existed. He was a real historical figure. Josephus, a non-Christian Jewish historian, wrote in AD 93:

> There was about this time Jesus, a wise man, if indeed we should call him a man; for he was a doer of marvellous deeds, a teacher of men who receive the truth with pleasure. He won over many Jews and also many Greeks. This man was the Messiah. And when Pilate had him condemned to the cross at the instigation of the leading men amongst us, those that loved him at first did not forsake him, for he appeared to them alive again the third day.

Jesus was born as a human baby.	Luke 2:6
He was a man with human emotions.	John 4:6
He was a leader, a teacher and a miracle-worker.	John 6:1–24
He was the Messiah.	John 4:25–26
He claimed to be God.	John 5:17–19
Others claimed that He was God.	John 1:1–4
Because Jesus is God, He (and no one else) can fill our God-shaped hole. None of us is perfect – we all miss the target of God's perfection.	Romans 3:23
The consequence of sin is spiritual and physical death. But the free gift of God is eternal life in Jesus Christ.	Romans 6:23
Jesus died in our place. In doing that He took away our sins, like a dustbin man taking away our rubbish.	2 Corinthians 5:21
Three days after His death on the cross, Jesus rose again.	1 Corinthians 15:3–4
If this is not true our faith is worthless.	1 Corinthians 15:17

Questions are often asked about the Resurrection: Did Jesus really die? Were the witnesses trustworthy? Did somebody hide the dead body? Did the disciples hallucinate? All of these questions can be answered if we believe the testimony of the eyewitnesses. They were certain they had seen Jesus alive, and later they died for saying that they had seen Him.   Luke 24:36–43

We know that Jesus is alive because He lives in us and through us.   John 14:19–20

The Holy Spirit
Who is He?
He is God.   Genesis 1:2; John 4:24
The Bible talks about God the Father, God the Son and God the Holy Spirit. H_2O has three forms – ice, water and steam. God is also three in one – Father, Son and Holy Spirit. The Holy Spirit was promised by Jesus as a helper and a teacher.   John 14:15–20

He is a guarantee of our future inheritance and the first instalment of all that God has planned for us.   Ephesians 1:13–14

What does He do?
He gives us God's new life.   John 3:5–8
He helps us to become like Jesus.   Galatians 5:22
He produces fruit in our lives.   Philippians 4:17
He unites us with other Christians into a new family – the Church.   Ephesians 4:3–4
He gives us power to serve God.   Acts 1:8
He gives many gifts to the Church.   1 Corinthians 12

The gifts are the tool-kit God has given us, so that we can be effective in His service.

Lifestyle

Jesus calls us to follow Him.   Matthew 4:19–20

This means that He is offering us a personal friendship and His own way of life.

Following Jesus is doing what He says, even if this means going in the opposite direction to everyone else.

Being a follower of Jesus is difficult.   Luke 9:23–24

Jesus gave up His life for us, and so we should give up our lives for Him. This means ending one way of life and starting a new one.

Jesus said that we are His witnesses or representatives.   Acts 1:8

Being a witness involves telling others about Jesus.

As we follow Jesus, we grow to be more like Him.

The work of Jesus continues today through Christians all over the world.   John 14:12–13

The Early Church met daily to worship God.   Acts 2:42–47

During this time of worship they did four things which we also need to do to stay close to Jesus:

1. They studied the apostles' teaching – for us this means learning from the Bible.

2. They shared fellowship – this means sharing your life with other Christians.
3. They broke bread together – this means remembering Jesus as we eat the bread and drink the wine at Holy Communion.
4. Prayer – this means talking and listening to God.

Like the four legs of a chair, these four things are all vital.